When I Die, Bury Me Well

When I Die, Bury Me Well

Death, Burial, Almsgiving, and Restoration
in the Book of Tobit

FRANCIS M. MACATANGAY

PICKWICK *Publications* · Eugene, Oregon

WHEN I DIE, BURY ME WELL
Death, Burial, Almsgiving, and Restoration in the Book of Tobit

Pickwick Publications
An Imprint of Wipf and Stock Publishers
199 W. 8th Ave., Suite 3
Eugene, OR 97401

www.wipfandstock.com

PAPERBACK ISBN: 978-1-4982-0985-4
HARDCOVER ISBN: 978-1-4982-0987-8
EBOOK ISBN: 978-1-4982-0986-1

Cataloguing-in-Publication data:

Names: Macatangay, Francis M.

Title: When I die, bury me well : death, burial, almsgiving, and restoration in the book of Tobit / Francis M. Macatangay.

Description: Eugene, OR: Pickwick Publications. | Includes bibliographic references and indexes.

Identifiers: ISBN 978-1-4982-0985-4 (paperback) | ISBN 978-1-4982-0987-8 (hardcover) | ISBN 978-1-4982-0986-1 (ebook)

Subjects: LCSH: Bible. Tobit—Criticism, interpretation, etc.

Classification: BS1725.52 M333 2016. (paperback) | BS1725.52 (ebook)

Manufactured in the U.S.A.   10/31/16

Dedicated to my parents, Ben and Medy,
my brother, Ferdinand, and sisters, Marizel, Mylene, and Marites
and
in a special way
to my uncle,
Fr. Tony Maramot

A man's dying is more the survivors' affair than his own.

—Thomas Mann, *The Magic Mountain*

God himself took a day to rest in, and a good man's grave is his Sabbath.

—John Donne

Contents

Preface

The Book of Tobit is a story of Jews living in exile told in fourteen short chapters. In Roman Catholic liturgy, the Book of Tobit is often encountered at weddings. Two brief passages from this deuterocanonical book, Tob 7:9–10, 11–15 and Tob 8:5–7, are sometimes chosen as the Old Testament reading for the celebration of the sacrament of marriage. The first passage recounts the scene where Tobiah requests for the hand of Sarah. Raguel, who is Sarah's father, explains to his future son-in-law the situation that has plagued his daughter in an attempt to discourage Tobiah from pursuing his plan. Tobiah will not be deterred, however. After much insistence on the part of Tobiah, Raguel gives in to Tobiah's demand and gives his daughter to him in marriage according to the Law of Moses. The second option, which seems to be often preferred than the first, is a prayer that Tobiah recites after the demon has been expelled from the wedding chamber. Curiously enough, the second selection from the lectionary does not mention that Tobiah's prayer was recited after the demon had left the bridal room. With the omission of this detail, the lectionary seems to agree that it is best to leave demons uninvited or at least unmentioned at weddings! In any case, what is often remembered of the Book of Tobit is the wedding that takes place between the two main characters, Tobiah and Sarah.

The Book of Tobit clearly has other important theological concerns. Upon closer investigation, the story in fact reflects the fertile ground of Second Temple Judaism. An aspect of the book that has not received much exposure and investigation is the narrative preoccupation with burial of the dead. In an important section of the story, Tobit instructs his son to provide him and his wife proper burial after their deaths. At the beginning of the story, Tobit refers to his activity of burying the dead while living away from his homeland. As the narrative concludes, Tobit and Tobiah's in-laws all receive the gift of burial. Burying the dead as a work of mercy is clearly prominent in the narrative. And yet, despite the fact that burying the dead is one of the corporal works of mercy in the Catholic tradition, the Book of Tobit is not proclaimed at the funeral liturgy. Perhaps, the Book of Tobit should be provided as an option at funeral liturgies to encourage active interest and engagement in this corporal work of mercy.

Why do we attend funerals? Why do we bury the dead? Funerals are often arranged by the loved ones of the departed in recognition of the unbreakable bonds of love even in death. With eulogies and homilies, funerals often commemorate and celebrate the life of the deceased. A funeral is a way to ritualize closure and express final farewell; it provides a process to tame the power of death and comfort the living. A funeral opens an avenue to share in grief and sorrow, to commend the dead to the tender mercies of God, and to articulate hopes in life beyond the grave. Of course, burying the dead can mean many things in different cultures, stories, and contexts. In the Book of Tobit, the practice of burying the dead is a definitive act of charity that is imbued with certain meaning. The following pages are an attempt to shed some light on the symbolic significance of sending the dead away through proper ritual according to the Book of Tobit. This book then is a focused reflection on the dynamics of death and burial as they relate to God's promises to his people according to the Book of Tobit.

The completion of this work owes much to many. My gratitude goes to those who offered insightful comments after an early and sketchy version of this study was presented as a research paper at the Annual Catholic Biblical Association Meeting a few years ago, especially Gary Anderson, Jeremy Corley, and Geoffrey Miller. A multitude of thanks also goes to Fran Serena and Teresa Stevenson for pointing out ways to ensure clarity of thought and expression. The librarians at Cardinal Beran Library, especially Amanda Renevier, deserve thanks for their generous assistance in locating needed books and articles. Good friends Jesus and Maria Bahena merit mention for their act of charity and kindness at a time of need. My gratitude also goes to Fr. Eli Lopez, my parochial vicar, for his understanding. Last but not least, a word of acknowledgment and thanks goes to all my teachers, professors, and students from whom I have had the great joy and privilege to listen and learn.

April 25, 2016
Feast of St. Mark the Evangelist

ABBREVIATIONS

AB	Anchor Bible
ABD	*Anchor Bible Dictionary.* Edited by David Noel Freedman. 6 vols. New York: Doubleday, 1992
Bib	*Biblica*
BN	*Biblische Notizen*
BO	Biblica et Orientalia
BZ	*Biblische Zeitschrift*
BZAW	Beihefte zur Zeitschrift für die alttestamentliche Wissenschaft
CBA	Catholic Biblical Association
CBQ	*Catholic Biblical Quarterly*
CBQMS	Catholic Biblical Quarterly Monograph Series
CEJL	Commentaries on Early Jewish Literature
DCLSt	Deuterocanonical and Cognate Literature Studies
DJD	Discoveries in the Judean Desert
ETL	*Ephemerides Theologicae Lovaniensis*
FoSub	Fontes et Subsidia ad Bibliam pertinentes
HUCA	*Hebrew Union College Annual*
JBL	*Journal of Biblical Literature*
JQR	*Jewish Quarterly Review*
JSJ	*Journal for the Study of Judaism*
JSJSup	Journal for the Study of Judaism Supplement
JSOTSup	Journal for the Study of the Old Testament Supplement
JSP	*Journal for the Study of the Pseudepigrapha*
LHB	Library of Hebrew Bible

LSTS	Library of Second Temple Studies
OBO	Orbis biblicus et orientalis
OBT	Overtures to Biblical Theology
OTM	Old Testament Message
OTS	Old Testament Studies
RevQ	*Revue de Qumran*
RHPR	*Revue d'Histoire et de Philosophie Religieuses*
SBL	Society of Biblical Literature
SBLDS	Society of Biblical Literature Dissertation Series
	SCS Septuagint Commentary Series
SJOT	*Scandinavian Journal of the Old Testament*
TDOT	*Theological Dictionary of the Old Testament*. Edited by G. Johannes Botterweck et al. 15 vols. Grand Rapids: Eerdmans, 1974–

PROLOGUE

In Philip Roth's award-winning 2007 novel titled *Everyman*, the unnamed protagonist, driving on the New Jersey turnpike and remembering that the exit to the Jewish cemetery south of Newark airport is near, finds a sudden urge to visit his parents' graves. While searching for their plot and recalling the memories of their funerals, he meets a gravedigger and prods him into a detailed disquisition about the nature of his work. He comes to an important insight on why the dead are buried at all. "They were just bones, bones in a box, but their bones were his bones, and he stood as close to the bones as he could, as though the proximity might link him up with them and mitigate the isolation born of losing his future and reconnect him with all that had gone."[1] In burying the dead and in providing graves for them, one can, in some uncanny way, reconnect and be with the dead; the memorialization keeps the living connected to what is most significant about the dearly departed, softening, disguising even, the separation between the living and the dead. The grave, in other words, keeps alive the ongoing relationship between the living and the dead.[2] The marked tomb articulates not only the social and visual presence of the dead within the living community but also the kinship that exists between the dead and their surviving progenies. In short, the grave provides a memorial and territorial expression to the enduring bonds between the dead and the living.

The Book of Tobit is a narrative renowned for its emphasis on the noble practice and corporal work of burying the dead. Other than Genesis perhaps, no other scriptural book or Second Temple text refers to burial of the dead more than the Book of Tobit. At the start of the story, Tobit refers to this act of charity. While under the rule of foreign kings, Tobit

---

1. Roth, *Everyman*, 170.
2. Harrison, *Dominion of the Dead*, 22–23.

would bury his dead kinsmen despite the threat of death (Tob 1:16–20; 2:1–8). At the end, the storyteller takes pains to point out twice that Tobit is buried with great honor (14:1, 11b), thus fulfilling his expressed desire for a proper burial (4:3). The narrator likewise notes the burial of Tobit's wife Hannah and Tobiah's parents in law, impressing upon the reader that all the members of the household receive a proper funeral. The burial of the dead serves as a narrative leitmotif that brackets the entire narrative arc. In the worldview of the story, burial of the dead is undeniably important.[3]

The primal epiphany of Roth's protagonist may speak to some of the concerns regarding burial of the dead in the Book of Tobit. Burying the dead is a practice that shines a spotlight on kinship affiliation or on the "link" that "reconnects" Tobit's fellow Israelites who are dead with the household of Israel. How does the Book of Tobit understand this link and reconnection and what are its implications? What claim does the activity of burial make in the Book of Tobit? By considering the book's emphasis on burying the dead in the context of Israelite burial ideology and interment practices, this short study is an attempt at a response.

Israel Abrahams noted more than a century ago that the frequency of references to this type of piety in the story begs for an explanation.[4] Some scholars contend that Tobit's burial of the dead shows his solidarity with his kinsmen.[5] To be sure, Tobit's interment activities underscore kinship relationship, suggesting that no member of the house of Jacob would leave this world without burial. Kinship, which is crucial in Tobit's world, endures, and burial expresses its permanence. And yet there are nonetheless very few studies on why death and burial are central in the story. I would like to propose that the significance of this leitmotif in the symbolic universe of the story lies in the mimetic and anticipatory functions of such a practice. The mimetic function of burying the dead lies in the hope that God will imitate Tobit's action of gathering the dead of Israel by burial in the sense that God will reward Tobit with a similar act of gathering dead Israel to the land. The mimetic is indicative of the anticipatory in that Tobit's charitable deed of burying the dead looks forward to God's greatest act of charity, which will be shown in his salvific activity of gathering and restoring the

---

3. See, for instance, Ego, "Death and Burial," 87; David, "Burial," 492; Moore, *Tobit*, 120, 130; Otzen, *Tobit*, 42.

4. Abrahams, "Tobit and Genesis," 349.

5. See Deselaers, *Buch Tobit*, 351–54; deSilva, *Introducing the Apocrypha*, 75; Rabenau, *Studien zum Buch Tobit*, 132–34.

whole household of Israel to the land. The Israelite ideology of interment will help bolster these claims, and the point about burial and kinship will prove significant to the argument here. Suffice it to say that in the context of the personal tragedies of Tobit and Sarah understood as refracting the deathly condition of exile, the practice of burying the dead ultimately points to Tobit's claim upon the land, and therefore, upon wholeness and life.

GENERAL ISSUES IN THE BOOK OF TOBIT

The Book of Tobit is set in the remote time of the Neo-Assyrian Empire during the siege and deportation of the northern kingdom of Israel in the eighth to seventh century (cf. 2 Kgs 15:29). The mention of "the prophets of Israel" (14:4), the direct quotation from Amos (2:6), and the references to the Book of Moses as ostensibly normative texts indicate, however, that Tobit was likely written at a date later than the FOURTH century BCE. Since Tobit shares some of the similar concerns as the Book of Sirach (e.g., Tob 4:4 and Sir 7:27–28; Tob 4:7–8, 16 and Sir 7:32–35; Tob 12:9 and Sir 3:30) but does not seem to reveal any awareness of the elements and circumstances suggestive of the Maccabean era, it is likely that a devout but unknown Jewish writer composed the story sometime between 225 and 175 BCE. Tobit reflects the condition of the Jews just before the Maccabean revolt, making this period the likely *terminus ad quem* for the book's writing. The Hebrew and Aramaic Qumran fragments of Tobit (4Q196–200) suggest that Tobit was being translated and copied at least by 100 BCE.

The place of Tobit's writing is difficult to ascertain. Some scholars suggest that a Diaspora Jew penned the story. In this case, some have posited an eastern Mediterranean provenance while others have proposed Alexandria, Egypt as its place of composition. In the mind of this author, it is likely that a Jewish author from the Land of Israel, perhaps one from somewhere north of Jerusalem, wrote the book. Two reasons can be proffered for this claim: first, Tobit is familiar with, or at least sympathetic to, certain halakhic practices found in the Land of Israel at that time, such as those attested at Qumran;[6] and, second, Tobit presents those living outside the land in exilic terms, betraying a view from the inside looking out, not from the outside looking in.[7] Like any settler or immigrant who finds a new home, a Jew and his descendants who had lived for a long period of time

6. See Dimant, "Tobit and Qumran Halakhah," 121–40.

7. See Macatangay, *Wisdom Instructions*, 285–86.

away from the homeland would not necessarily regard their existence as exilic. The residents of the land would be more likely to espouse a view of their fellow countrymen abroad as exilic.

The Book of Tobit is a mosaic of varied literary traditions. The author weaves biblical and non-biblical threads to create a fabric that is the story of Tobit. Folktales and Greek legends are alleged to have influenced the shape of the narrative. For the most part, however, the Jewish biblical tradition seemed to have been the primary source of inspiration for the Book of Tobit, the major concern of which is to address the folly of exile evident in the incongruity between the divine promise of land and the dispersion of the Jews. Since the story evokes, recycles, and adapts antecedent scriptural traditions and literary texts of Israel, the alert reader has to keep one eye on the Old Testament to better appreciate the narrative and its claims. The story is crafted with Israel's scriptural heritage in mind. To cite an example, Tobit's character in his first person narration is developed according to scriptural principles and deuteronomistic ideals (cf. Gen 15:6; 22:1; Deut 6:17–18). One can thus imagine this anonymous but devout Jewish author working at his beat-up wooden desk, dipping his pen in many inkpots,[8] recasting and alluding to various streams of Jewish traditions and literary heritage in order to respond creatively through a story to the theological conundrums posed by the continued scattering of the Jews. Frank Zimmermann is correct in asserting that "in the loom of the Tobit tale, the woof comes from the folklore of mankind, and the warp and the pattern, the vitality and the color come from the religious experience of the Jewish people."[9]

Perhaps because of the eclecticism of the literary traditions embedded in the book, the narrative integrity of the work has been questioned. In fact, some have posited that the story achieved its present form after a long process of redaction, expansions, and interpolations. Narrative inconsistencies, such as the seemingly opposing claims of Tob 2:1 and 1:20, are alleged to reveal editorial revisions. Some narrative seams are often cited as major reasons. First, there is the sudden change from first-person narration in the beginning of the story to third-person in Tob 3:6. Irene Nowell, however, has shown that both narrations share the same style and omniscient point

8. Nickelsburg, "Tobit's Mixed Ancestry," 348. See also Machiela and Perrin, "Tobit and the Genesis Aporcyphon," 116-17.

9. Zimmermann, *Book of Tobit*, 12. For a survey of recent scholarship on Tobit in the last decade, see Perrin, "An Almanac of Tobit Studies," 107–42.

of view.[10] Additionally, the change of voice that allows the fusion of autobi-ographical discourse with biblical ideals is also not uncommon in Qumran Aramaic texts that are contemporaneous with the Book of Tobit.[11] Second, the final two chapters, Tob 13–14, with its eschatological tone and focus on the future of Jerusalem and the restoration of Israel, seem unnecessary and out of place after Tob 12, which can easily function as the conclusion of the work. Lawrence Wills remarks that with these additions, "the spirited novel of chapters 2–12 has become heavily laden with theological pretension."[12] This estimation, however, does not take into account the fact that there might be a theological design that embraces the final chapters. Even when the narrative comes to its calm, there is still a certain "tension and fore-boding" that looms.[13] This requires that the ending be taken seriously for these final chapters may reveal the "theological intention" or the allusive purpose behind the work.[14] Certainly, the many allusions to familiar texts and traditions in the narrative enhance the organic unity of the story while the problem of exile pulls all the other literary and theological elements in the narrative into a cohesive whole.[15] In sum, it appears likely that the Book of Tobit as it has come down to us possesses a literary integrity and a theological unity.

The transmission history and the manuscript tradition of Tobit are complex. Originally written in a Semitic language, most likely Aramaic, the work was handed on in a number of translations of varying textual nature.[16] The book is preserved in three Greek text-types. The long Greek version is found in codex *Sinaiticus* while the short version, which is typically con-sidered a revision and abridgement of the long one, survives primarily in the *Alexandrinus* and the *Vaticanus*. The third text-type is attested in some Greek cursive manuscripts such as 106 (6:9—12:22) and the *Syro-Hexapla*

---

10. Nowell, "Narrator in the Book of Tobit," 29; *Narrative Technique*, 161–62. Perrin ("Tobit's Context and Contacts," 23–51) notes that Tobit shares this preference for the first person voice with other Aramaic texts found at Qumran.

11. See Perrin, "Tobit's Context and Contacts," 27–32.

12. Wills, *The Jewish Novel*, 91.

13. Macatangay, *Wisdom Instructions*, 128.

14. Kiel, *Rethinking Retribution*, 23. See also Weitzmann, "Allusion," 49–61.

15. See Macatangay, *Wisdom Instructions*, 7–43.

16. On the theological and literary resemblances between the Book of Tobit and other Aramaic texts at Qumran, see Perrin, "Tobit's Context and Contacts," 23–51. See also Machiela and Perrin, "Tobit and the Genesis Apocryphon," 111–32.

(7:11—12:22).[17] These text-types may be regarded as witnesses to a common textual tradition and not necessarily as different and competing recensions.[18] Four Aramaic and one Hebrew fragments of Tobit were also found at Qumran (4Q196–200).[19] Many scholars believe that the long Greek version in the *Sinaiticus* enjoys textual priority because of its textual proximity to the Qumran fragments of Tobit.

The translation of the Book of Tobit from Aramaic into Hebrew, Greek and Latin, attests to the work's broad appeal and wide regard. Specifically, the presence of the Book of Tobit at Qumran confirms its popularity; the Qumran community deemed the text as worthy of being read, studied, collected, and preserved in its library. As to why Tobit enjoyed certain esteem at Qumran, it has been suggested, quite ambiguously, that the claims of the story share the basic Essene ideals with the Qumran community.[20] It is more likely, however, that Tobit's religious piety and practices while in exile bear a significant correspondence with those espoused by several Qumranic texts. One should also not disregard Tobit's robust attention to proper covenantal conduct in terms of righteousness and truth, along with its theological tendencies towards predeterminism, as factors for the work's strong appeal among the residents of Qumran. That Tobit also shares with other Aramaic literature at Qumran a concern for the ancestral instruction of religious duties, an insistence on endogamous marriage, and an eschatological vision of the New Jerusalem might also explain why Tobit is valued at the caves of Qumran.[21]

In the end, the Book of Tobit is an edifying story that delights with the elements of humor, irony, romance, and adventure.[22] It is clear, however, that one of its chief purposes is didactic. With ethical and sapiential materials in Tobit 4, 12, and 14, the author aims to reinforce a certain set of values.

---

17. See Hanhart, *Tobit*, 31–36; Wagner, *Polyglotte Tobit-Synopse*, xx–xxiii; Weeks et al., *The Book of Tobit*, 10–20.

18. See Weeks, "Restoring the Greek Tobit," 1–15, noting that "*Sinaiticus* is one witness to a text-type, not the embodiment of that type, and its text of Tobit is riddled with errors and omissions" (2); Weeks, "Reconstructing Tobit," 35–47.

19. See Fitzmyer, "Tobit," 1–76.

20. See, for example, Fröhlich, "Tobit against the Background of the Dead Sea," 69–70.

21. See Perrin, "Tobit's Context and Contacts," 23–51.

22. On irony, see Moore, *Tobit*, 24–26. See also Macatangay, "Μισθός and Irony," 576–84. On the comic aspects, see McCracken, "Narration and Comedy," 401–18. See also Pyper, "Kierkegaard's Reading of Tobit," 59–71.

The Book of Tobit was likely intended as an unconventional manual for creating a habit of being for Jews living in the dispersion; it was meant to prescribe and form a distinct identity around the religious ethos of truth, charity, and righteousness for those living far away from home.

More importantly, the story contains a Diaspora-directed message that inspires well-founded hopes of return to and repossession of the land. The book presents itself as a "written record" or an acknowledgment of God's marvelous work of restoring Tobit and his household into life. The end in view is to enliven Israel's hopes of renewal in the land (12:20). It is the contention of this study that the burial motif in the story reinforces the message of restoration of Israel to the land. Indeed, the narrative views the practice of burial as a great act of mercy. And yet, there is a complex of ideas associated with burying the dead that, when viewed against the horizon of the narrative universe, makes it likely that burial is associated more with hopes of restoration and repossession of the land after exile than with respect or any pious practice typically reserved for the dead. Put succinctly, burying the dead in the Book of Tobit is about trusting in a divine promise.

1

THE BOOK OF TOBIT
AS A NARRATIVE OF EXILE

THE BOOK OF TOBIT is a delightful narrative that recounts the vicissitudes of Jewish life in exile. In fact, the problem of exile is what makes this work cohere as a narrative, if not an ancient novel. The exile is the larger plot around whose gravity the subplots involving the misfortunes of Tobit and Sarah revolve. The state of separation from the land is the main suffering in which the individual afflictions of the main characters participate.[1] If absence is a kind of presence, then the absence of a homeland is a presence that haunts the story of Tobit.

From a structural point of view, the condition of exile is the decisive deficit that awaits narrative resolution.[2] Indeed, despite the denouement of the story in Tobit 12 where Raphael discloses the divine hand behind the events that have led to the healing of Tobit's blindness and the wedding

---

1. Collins, "Judaism," 28, is certainly correct in claiming that exile, though an undesirable situation, is not the factor that drives Tobit to despair and desire for death in his prayer. However, the implication of this observation that exile is not the overriding concern of the narrative misses the point. In Fassbeck, "Tobit's Religious Universe," 192–93, the claim that the Diaspora setting is a mere literary device is misleading. Levine, "Diaspora as Metaphor," 106, is right in assessing the problems in the narrative as arising out of the Diaspora context. Ego ("The Book of Tobit and the Diaspora," 41) comments that the spatial perspective makes it clear that the story is to be read as a "Diaspora story focusing on the existence of Israelites in the exile." See also Rauntenberg, *Verlässlikchkeit des Wortes*, 17–20.

2. See Soll, "Misfortune and Exile," 209–31.

of Tobiah to Sarah, the unremitting misfortune of exile still remains to be tackled and resolved. Only in Tobit's hymn of praise in Tobit 13 and in his farewell speech in Tobit 14, both inspired by the hopes based on the providential events that sort out the conflicts in the story, does the reader get a confident hint at a future ingathering and restoration contingent on God's initiative of mercy. Indeed, both chapters anticipate the positive closure to the narrative shortfall previously disclosed in the beginning of the book (1:3).

From a theological point of view, the problem of exile also exerts its pull upon the narrative coherence of the book as Tobit takes on the discombobulating divorce between history and the divine word. God has promised his chosen people a land of milk and honey where life is in abundance and yet, Tobit's situation, in spite of his fidelity, speaks otherwise. Despite such a split, however, God's order and control is firmly in place and divine providence is still active, since "nothing escapes his hand" (13:2).[3] In short, the problem of exile governs the narrative and the effects of exile on the individual vis-à-vis the community greatly affect the chronological and theological struggles in Tobit.[4] This chapter explores the symbolization of exile as death in the story.

EXILE AS METAPHOR FOR THE DIASPORA

The story of Tobit is set in the Assyrian exile, which the writer seemed to have employed as the lens to view Jewish life in the dispersion. Around the time the Book of Tobit was written (ca. third and second century BC), there were many Jews who lived dispersed outside the homeland. Despite provisions to resettle in the land of their ancestors, there were many who chose to reside and make a life in newfound lands. In time, the sense of belonging and loyalty to the land diminished. It is likely that many of those outside the land did not see themselves as deportees. For them, the state of being in exile has ceased.[5] Despite setting the story of Tobit in the historical

---

3. For a discussion of how the narrative suspense relates to divine providence and Tobit's theological take on Diaspora existence, see Schellenberg, "Suspense," 315–20.

4. Cousland, "A Comedy in Error," 545, notes that a comic reading of Tobit not only undermines Tobit's moral authority but also "trivializes the exile."

5. Collins, *Between Athens and Jerusalem*, 3, remarks that Jews in the Hellenistic Diaspora "were no longer exiles against their will; their exile was no longer a cause of derision."

reality of the Assyrian captivity in the eighth century, the experience of exile as such has become the metaphor for the condition of living abroad. Residence outside the land is understood to be exilic. The book was thus composed at a distance from the momentous event of exile, giving this work the distinction of being one of the earliest documented perspectives on Diaspora Jews from the inside looking out.

In the opening verses of the story, the third-person narrator alludes to the fall of Samaria, the capital of the Northern Kingdom (1:1–2). The narrator does not say where Tobit and his tribe were forced into exile. It is only later that Tobit in first person voice identifies Nineveh as the place of his captivity (1:10). After his eyes were opened, Tobit exclaimed that there was great rejoicing among the Jews in Nineveh (11:18). This claim is anachronistic since those who were deported to Nineveh are referred to in 2 Kgs 18:11 as children of Israel and never as Jews or Judeans.[6] This indicates that Tobit reflects the situation of the dispersion rather than the Assyrian exile. Moreover, Tobit's use of the term "to scatter" or "to disperse" in his prayer (3:6), in his praise (13:3–6), and in his farewell discourse (14:4), describes what may well be the current reality of the Jews in the story. His prayer in particular claims that God has scattered his people among the nations (3:4).

Traditional narratives begin in a state of calm, which is soon disturbed by conflicts and problems that are later fixed, returning the story to its original calm. Tobit does not enjoy this initial calm. The only sense of calm comes from the listing of Tobit's genealogy (1:1). Otherwise, Tobit's story starts with a reference to captivity (1:2), and the story is replete with conflicts and troubles for the protagonists until the very end. Even then, the sense of finality is tentative and a true happy ending is only hinted at.

The opening verses of the narrative do not identify the place of Tobit's captivity. The absence of the name of the place where Tobit and his co-religionists spend their exilic fate is intriguing. With a rather detailed list of names that traces Tobit's blood lineage and a list of names that identifies the topography of the land affiliation of Tobit and his tribe, one expects a mention of the place of captivity to where the tribe of Naphtali was taken. Such, however, is not the case. Despite the meticulous care the narrator devotes to Tobit's genealogy and place of origin, the strange land to which Tobit's tribe was taken remains unnamed. Either the trauma of exile has blocked the memory of the place or its distinct absence serves a specific fictive function. This lack, of course, creates a glaring gap in the list of topographical

6. See Zimmermann, *The Book of Tobit*, 16; Zappella, *Tobit*, 116.

references and implies that exile is a denial or negation of place.[7] Tobit and his tribe's location are not their own; naming the locale would give it a historical referent or existence, as if to say that place is a reality in the story. In the same sense that time can feel less like a ticking clock and more like a condition, so too is that other coordinate of reality called space. Here then, the absence of a geographical location has become a state of being, a mode of existing.

To withhold such a significant piece of information means that Tobit's place of exile enjoys a literary function more than anything else; indeed, exile has become the root metaphor for the general experience of life in the dispersion.[8] The unidentified location of Tobit's exile becomes a *modus dicendi* that tries to capture the state of dispersion; it is a way of understanding Diaspora living. In fact, Tobit's first-person repeated use of the word "captivity" along with its cognates (1:3,10) focuses and defines the contour of his character. Exile then is no longer a simple reference to the historical deportation of the northern tribes by the Assyrians but a symbolic description of the dispersed status of God's people.

Exile is no longer an historical event. Exile has become a narrative code and metaphor for the Diaspora and the meanings associated with exile are now mapped on to the view of life in the Diaspora. Metaphors, of course, suggest something of one thing in terms of another. Meanings or senses that are usually attached to a thing or experience are applied to another in order to comprehend and experience one reality in terms of another.[9] The use of metaphors produces a gestalt that facilitates understanding of the thing or experience to which the metaphor is applied. And so, the Book of Tobit grafts the connotations that exile evokes on to the circumstance and experience of life outside the land. Thus, exile is not only the chronic

---

7. See Ego, "'Heimat in der Fremde,'" 270–83; "The Book of Tobit and the Diaspora," 41–44. See also Haag, "Das Tobitbuch und die Tradition von Jaweh," 27. Levine, "Diaspora as Metaphor," 107, notes that Tobiah's journey with Raphael to find a bride replaces Tobit's pilgrimage to Jerusalem, giving the impression that "a genealogical focus replaces a geographical one." This remark could also apply to Tob 1:1–2 where genealogy as identifier takes precedence over geography. Oeming observes that Tobit shows the influence of the Chronicler's theological ideals and criteria for inclusion in the "true Israel" with its genealogy, observance of Torah, and loyalty to the house of David and the Jerusalem Temple ("Jewish Identity," 550–52).

8. Kiel ("Tobit and Moses Redux," 97) notes that life outside the land is "ciphered in the book as the exile." See also Otzen, *Tobit and Judith*, 43.

9. On this point, see Lakoff and Johnson, *Metaphors We Live By*, 5.

misfortune in the story but the root metaphor from which other sensory images in the narrative emanate.

The Book of Tobit exploits, for example, the image of "the road,"[10] to portray the volatility of the Diaspora situation. The major characters in the story are on the road; they live a precarious existence and do not enjoy any measure of stability. The road is unsafe (1:15) and only an angel of God knows all the roads (5:6). Tobit is in constant motion (1:14–15, 19, 22). His prayer for death is a sign of his desire to find an eternal home and thus a final rest from constant movement (3:2–6). In fact, the central section with Tobiah and Raphael from Tobit 5–11 is but a long story of being on the road. Since the roads are unfamiliar, even dangerous, only an angelic traveling guide and companion can navigate the way in strange lands and ensure passage to safe shores. As the story returns to some form of calm, Tobit insists before dying that Tobiah and his family leave Nineveh for Media (14:3–4). In a dispersed state, it is understandable that the characters do not live "the reality of the place but of the road,"[11] journeying into and out of places. In a way, the narrative gives off a kinetic sense in that almost everyone is on the move, pointing to further departures. Even as the story concludes, the reader attains an eschatological vision of everyone journeying to Jerusalem in the plenitude of time. Set in exile, the story radiates neither a sense of rootedness nor a confidence in belonging to a place. That Tobit belongs to the tribe of Naphtali, one of the lost tribes, is a further clue to his geographical instability.[12] With motion as the story's reality, the sense of estrangement from a place pervades the narrative.

The experiences of exile and blindness are both pivotal plot points in the story. In his prayer of despair in Tob 3:1–6, Tobit identifies himself with errant Israel despite his personal piety, innocence, and righteousness. As a representative of his own people, Tobit views his blindness as a sign of God's reproof for infidelity (cf. Deut 28:28–29; Isa 59:9–10).[13] Blindness, of course, is a biblical image often associated with exile (Isa 29:18).

As a narrative of the dispersion, Tobit draws furthermore from the biblical portrayal of the exilic experience. In the land of captivity, the

10. Desaelers (*Das Buch Tobit,* 343–48) considers "the way" an important *Leitwortstil* in the narrative.

11. Jensen ("Family, Fertility and Foul Smell," 138–39) also notes that "the traditional place-oriented mentalities have been replaced by structures, connections, and junctions" (138).

12. Levine, "Diaspora as Metaphor," 107.

13. See Macatangay, "Exile as Metaphor," 183. See also Gafni, *Land,* 19–40.

tongues of Tobit's neighbors lash him like whips for continuing his practice of burying the dead despite the royal decree; he is a byword for reproach, derision, and mockery (2:8; 3:4). Sarah's maids also insult her with verbal abuse (3:7–9). In the scriptural world, to be an object of reproach and horror points to the experience of exile (cf. Bar 2:4; Deut 28:37; Psalm 44:13; Jer 24:9; 29:18; 2 Chron 7:20). The ridicule and mockery that Tobit and Sarah experience from their Gentile neighbors place their exilic circumstance in stark relief. The *Letter of Aristeas* agrees with the disgrace of deportation depicted in the story of Tobit. Questioned as to how to express patriotism, the sage responds: "Keep in mind that it is good to live and die in one's country. Residence abroad brings contempt upon poor men, and upon rich—disgrace, as though they were in exile for some wickedness." (*Ep. Aris* 249).

To be in exile is to experience the vagaries of life in the midst of the nations. The fact of the continued state of dispersion hovers over the story as an overwhelming misfortune. Tobit has admittedly an ambivalent, even complex, attitude toward exile.[14] Still, the notion that exile is an experience of death, a descent into darkness, seems paramount in the narrative. Of course, the story does not view death as annihilation nor a cessation of vital and biological functions but debility.

EXILE AS AN EXPERIENCE OF DEATH

The Book of Tobit is set outside the land that is construed as an existential locus of suffering and death. While living away from the homeland but not necessarily apart from God, the two families of Tobit and Raguel suffer heartbreaking misfortunes. Tobit becomes blind and impoverished despite his righteous acts and fidelity to God's law. Like Job, Tobit suffers as a righteous man and wishes for death (3:1–6; cf. Job 3:11–16; 6:8–9).

In Nineveh, changes in the political climate are like stormy winds that buffeted Tobit. When he was reported to the king for the stealth taking and burial of dead Israelite bodies, the king wanted to put him to death, issuing a warrant for his arrest for violating the royal decree.[15] In fear, he fled and

14. Albertz, *Israel in Exile*, 30. See also Macatangay, "Exile as Metaphor," 183–92, for the various connotations of exile in the story.

15. See Gafni, *Land*, 22–23: "Jews living outside of Judea constantly lived with the fear that they might be punished by the ruling government for the sins of their brethren still residing in their perceived homeland. The author of the book of Tobit (1:18)

left his post as court purchaser. Though only flight would preserve Tobit's life from execution at this point, the possibility of death would nonetheless continue to be a haunting nightmare. The king confiscated his properties and Tobit became destitute. By a stroke of good luck, however, the king was assassinated and his son Esarhaddon ascended the throne (1:18–20). Since his nephew Ahiqar was second in command in Esarhaddon's court, Tobit was able to return to Nineveh where his son Tobiah and his wife Hannah were restored to him (2:1). Still, the presence of dead bodies on the streets of Nineveh (2:3–7) is a strong reminder of the continual threat of death.[16] This narrative sketch gives the impression that life under foreign rule is vulnerable and oppressive. Tobit and his family live in a zone where power can upend the established order and life is under the ubiquitous threat of random, windblown, and senseless events.

Life in exile does not only subject Tobit to the caprices and threats of foreign kings but also to the chances and whims of nature. After burying the body of a dead compatriot, Tobit rested in the courtyard and fell asleep, unaware of the birds atop the wall. Avian droppings fell on his eyes and white films developed over them, making him blind (3:9–10). As whimsical and random a narrative touch as that may seem, birds and their discharges prove to be a threat to Tobit's life. Tobit was afflicted with blindness for which no doctor was able to find a cure. The performance of a charitable deed has led to Tobit's loss of eyesight. As a consequence, he was unable to provide for his family and his wife Hannah worked for hire at weaving cloth. When Hannah came home from work with a young goat, Tobit's questioning of his wife ended in acrimony. Even the home has ceased to be the refuge of stability necessary for a good life to flourish.[17] With these tribulations, Tobit's balance is knocked precariously off-kilter. Tobit can no longer bear life's burdens nor exert any influence over nor expect any security from his environment. Hence, he utters a prayer in despair asking God to take his life and send him to his everlasting home (3:6). Tobit truly feels the fragility of his existence in exile; life as a captive is never a sinecure.

---

considered it only natural that Sennacherib, after his setback in Jerusalem, would vent his anger on the Jews of Nineveh; Tobit himself was forced to flee after burying the Jewish victims of the king's wrath."

16. Nowell, *Narrative Technique*, 203, notes that in the long Greek text-type, the verses that refer to death or burial constitute almost 22 percent of the book's 244 verses.

17. See for instance the analysis of the narrative's familial problems in Petraglio, "Tobit e Anna," 385–402.

A gradual series of unfortunate events has made the threat of death real, rendering Tobit as one who is death-bound. In the land of strangers, danger lurks.[18] If there is any break, luck or chance to prosper at all, it is fleeting. Under sovereign powers, Tobit's life is stripped bare and becomes, in fact, dispensable. Tobit has become blind and poor; he is an isolated man whose family could barely eke out a decent existence. Even as Tobit sends his only son to retrieve the deposited money to secure the family, his wife views his decision as letting go in old age the "staff of their hands" (5:18);[19] from her perspective, Tobit's decision seals their fate of death. No wonder then that when Tobit meets Raphael for the first time, he counts himself among the dead, claiming that he is "like the dead who no longer see the light" (5:10). Without the light, Tobit sleeps the sleep of death (cf. Ps. 13:3–4). In the arbitrary world of nature and in the oppressive climate of politics, Tobit hangs by a thread and lives a state of death while alive.[20] A world that is out of joint accords Tobit neither stability nor security.

The struggle with the forces of death continues unabated in Tobit's decision to entrust his son with a perilous mission. The destitution of his family, of course, causes Tobit to send his son to retrieve a sizable sum of money deposited with a cousin. Just as famine took Abraham and Sarah, and later, Jacob's sons to Egypt, poverty has forced Tobit to risk his son on a journey to Ecbatana to provide his family financial safety. The risky roads imply the likely loss of his son. With poverty and the possible loss of his son, the survival of the family is threatened. If Tobiah meets some disaster on this perilous journey, if Tobit's only son dies, as Hannah fears (Tob 5:18–20), his death would send his parents down to the grave in sorrow (Tob 6:15). Tobit and Hannah would not only have no one to bury them but they would also lose all reasonable expectations for survival and the continuation of their identities after their death. Hannah's complaint

18. See Albertz, *Israel in Exile*, 32: "They are defenseless against attacks by the local populace and arbitrary acts of those in power. They are killed like criminals in the public street, and no one cares." Oeming observes, "They are punished for their success with harsh and inhuman penalties, such as the prohibition to bury the dead" ("Jewish Identity," 547).

19. For a discussion of the history and significance of this phrase, see Betrand, "'Un baton de vieillesse'," 33–37. For a metaphorical analysis of the phrase as it relates to the narrative and character development, see Macatangay, "Metaphors and the Character Construction of Tobiah," 75–86.

20. Albertz (*Israel in Exile*, 32) notes that those living outside the land "are defenseless against attacks by the local populace and arbitrary acts of those in power. They are killed like criminals in the public street, and no one cares."

against Tobit's decision recalls Jacob's lament that if Benjamin were to be taken away from him and if something were to happen to him, his white head will be sent down to Sheol in grief (Gen 42:36–38). The possibility of losing their only son can likewise spell death for Tobit and Hannah.

The family of Raguel has its own problems. Sarah, Raguel's daughter, remains without a husband despite her beauty, innocence, and trustworthiness (3:14–15; 6:12). Her attempts to secure a husband in marriage failed seven times. The jealous Asmodeus killed each of the seven men on their wedding night before the marriage could be consummated, leaving Sarah childless and seven times a widow.[21] Needless to say, an absent or dead husband poses a threat to Sarah's well-being and flourishing. Without a husband to provide her security and protection, Sarah has and is nothing; she has neither child nor opportunities to perpetuate the family line. She has lost the possibility to bear children not because of infertility, as is the case with the matriarchs and barren women in scriptures, but because all her husbands are deceased. The lack of a husband and child implies that Sarah is practically dead with neither worth or reason for living.

With seven dead husbands, Sarah becomes a sociological misfit mocked and verbally abused (Tob 3:7–10). She has lost her honorable reputation and standing before a community of eligible bachelors, making her unmarriageable (cf. 6:14–15). Her chances of acquiring a husband have been reduced to nil. Taunted by her maids, Sarah is virtually at the end of her wits; fate seems to have consigned her to non-existence at the prime of her life. Her consequent lack of honor puts her on the cusp of social death. And so, she feels that it would be better for her to hang herself. Concerned however that her death will cause her father to go down to the netherworld in sorrow, Sarah changes her mind and begs God in prayer to take her from the face of the earth instead (cf. 3:15).[22]

The fates of Tobit and Sarah parallel each other.[23] Their stories are narratives of weakened and friable lives. The threat of non-existence from a political and natural plane in the case of Tobit corresponds to the threat from the supernatural sphere in the case of Sarah. While Tobit suffers the threat of death from his political and natural environments, Sarah bears

21. Hicks-Keeton ("Already/Not Yet," 107) observes the irony in the meaning of Sarah's name and her situation, claiming that "the demon Asmodeus is more in control of Sarah's ('Mistress') life than she is, depriving her of the ability to be a proper mistress."

22. Kierkegaard says of Sarah: "I have read much sorrow but I doubt if anywhere there is a sorrow as deep as that residing in the life of that girl" (*Fear and Trembling*, 125).

23. See Nickelsburg, *Jewish Literature*, 30; Ego, *Buch Tobit*, 885–86.

the danger from another setting, the realm of the demonic. Interestingly, the birds whose droppings cover Tobit's eyes into blindness also insinuate demonic aura.[24] The presence of demons in the world of Tobit and Sarah may have something to do with their place of captivity. In fact, a tradition in a Second Temple Zion song contrasting the destinies of Babylon and Jerusalem found in Baruch and inspired by the prophetic oracle against Babylon in Isa 13:21 claims that the land of the nations that took Israel captive will be inhabited by demons (cf. Bar 4:35). Their experiences signal such a reality. In any event, the threats to life's flourishing stem from all sides. They come "only from outsiders"[25] and they all coalesce to weaken the welfare of the characters.

As the narrative threads the conflicts that beset Tobit and Sarah, the threats to non-existence expand then from the political to the social through the natural and ultimately to the supernatural. Oppression in exile extends its reach from all spheres; all realms, it seems, collude to make life of those in exile expendable and subject to the whims of various negative forces. In such a situation, those in exile can literally disintegrate and decompose like dead bodies strewn on Gentile streets.[26] Tobit's encounter with dead Jewish bodies transforms his exilic surroundings into a virtual abode for the dead.

The afflictions of Tobit and Sarah portend the haunting specter of death in the story. Such reality bubbles on to the narrative surface in and through their losses. While in exile, Tobit loses his eyesight, his source of income, and everything he holds dear. Sarah, on the other hand, loses seven husbands and the happiness and security that a husband can provide her. In other words, their distressing losses participate in a loss that is greater, namely the loss of a homeland. The tragic experiences of Tobit and Sarah are a function of exile in that their unfortunate situations simply reflect their alienation. Their fragility and weakened situations point to a much greater debilitation that is the exile. In other words, their sufferings are exile in miniature.

Would Tobit and Sarah have come to such adversities if they were in the land? It is certainly possible. After all, no one is free from the caprices

---

24. See Macatangay, "Apocalypticism and Narration," 212. See also Nickelsburg, *Jewish Literature*, 349n69.

25. See Pitkänen, "Family Life," 109.

26. See, for instance, van Unnik, *Selbstverständnis der Jüdischen Diaspora*, 149–50, where he argues that Diaspora is not a geographical referent but the disintegration of the whole into small, individual parts.

of nature and demons.[27] The vicissitudes of life visit an individual without respect for place or location. For one thing, ominous avian discharges and demons can certainly be encountered in the homeland. And yet, from the beginning of Tobit's story, there is a distinct insistence on Tobit's deportation to Nineveh, the land of the Assyrians. As the narrative concludes, the fact of exile looms large. The narrative begins and ends with the reality of exile. This specific setting colors the reading of the events that unfold within the timeline of the story; such narrative context is bound to influence the interpretation. In fact, Tobit's uncertain lot in the royal court that opens the narrative anticipates the unkind hands of fate that later await him in the story. There is a correlation, indirect though it may be, that a reader infers from the initial narrative situation of exile to the individual misfortunes that have befallen Tobit and Sarah. That reference to exile brackets the stories of personal tragedies demands a hermeneutic that prioritizes and engages the exilic experience. Otherwise, if exile does not act as an interpretive factor in the turn of events that brought misery to the families of Tobit and Raguel, it would be rather difficult to explain why the author insists on it from the very start of the story. If it were not the case, exile would have to be viewed as nothing but an arbitrary setting that has nothing to do whatsoever with the rest of what happens. The experience of separation from the land sets in motion the narrative arc of the story, which, in turn, creates the impression that only residence in the homeland provides safety.

A story is often propelled to dramatic greatness by its specificity; its universal appeal lies in its peculiarity. The parochial is paradoxically the royal road to the universal. Like any great drama, the Book of Tobit specifies and concretizes in and through the specific hardships of Tobit and Sarah the general experience of exile. The narrative employs the colors of death as refracted by and through the individual sufferings of Tobit and Sarah to paint what exile is like. In their particular afflictions, the narrative drama radiates a universal sense of what it means to be in exile—it is an experience of death. In their individual catastrophes, the story seems to say that if alienation from the homeland were a tureen of trauma, it is best allotted by the spoonful.

In some of the exilic prophets, one finds the view that exile is an unhurried road to death (cf. Jer 8:3; 17:14; Ezek 6:8–10; 12:4–6). Much later, Philo would express the sentiment that banishment from the land is "not

---

27. But see Collins ("Judaism," 28): "Presumably, sparrow droppings were no more of a hazard in the Diaspora than they were in the land of Israel."

the end but the beginning of other new misfortunes and entails in the place of one death which puts an end to pains a thousand deaths in which we do not lose sensation."[28] Such a statement endorses the view that exile poses oppressive threats to life and they come from all corners. Assimilation to the environment is no guarantee that such threats will disappear. For this reason, the story stresses endogamy with its promise of land inheritance as a way to avoid sterility and to combat death. It is hardly surprising that the demon Asmodeus, who threatens the life-giving marriage of Tobiah and Sarah, is an alien character, the Total Other,[29] who bears no kinship to Tobit. Asmodeus is paradigmatic of the threat that strange lands present to Jewish life and identity.

The Book of Tobit contains not only death-related images but also metaphorical death language. In his prayer, Tobit asks God to allow him to go from the face of the earth into dust (3:6). In his discourse, Tobit describes God as having the power to raise up and to cast down to the deepest recesses of the nether world (4:19). He compares his blindness as being among the dead where God's sunlight does not reach (5:10). In his hymn of praise, Tobit declares that God "casts down to the depths of the nether-world and brings up from the great abyss" (13:2).

Tobit's use of διασκορπίζω or "to scatter" in his prayer (3:1–6), in his hymn of praise (13:3–6), and in his farewell discourse (14:4) to describe the reality that God has dispersed his people among the nations may also shed light on the connection between death and exile. According to Willem van Unnik, the word "diaspora," which comes from διασκορπίζω or "to disperse," denotes the dissolution and disintegration of the whole into small individual parts.[30] Thus, to be dispersed is for Israel to be friable, to dissipate, disintegrating and decomposing in foreign lands. To be dispersed is thus to die. Tobit's burial activities make this all the more evident. When the king forbids the burial of the dead, it is an assertion that the deaths of these Jewish victims mean nothing; their deaths are not a loss. On the other hand, Tobit's burial of the dead affirms that someone significant has indeed been lost. Every burial means a loss for Israel and each loss attests to the gradual disintegration of Israel.

The Book of Tobit conforms to the Israelite understanding that death is "the weakest form of life," a "disorder" and "the most severe of illnesses

28. Philo, *On Abraham* 64.

29. See Ego, "Denn er liebt sie," 315.

30. van Unnik, *Selbsverständnis der Jüdischen Diaspora*, 149–50.

characterized by debilitation and physical fragility."[31] Death refers to the phenomena of brokenness, separation, and suffering. Death is anything that "detracts from the full potential" intended by God for his people.[32] For Tobit and Sarah, death is everything that limits their lives. The faces of death include blindness, poverty, and loss of husbands and of the possibility of children—conditions that have made them truly asthenic. The misfortunes of Tobit and Sarah thus create the impression that exile has pushed them to enervation, zapped of vitality. In the end, exile subverts God's creative and life-giving intentions for his people.

PRAYERS FOR DEATH

Tobit and Sarah wish for death seemingly as easily as sunflowers long for the sun. Tobit's prayerful lament exudes a pervasive sense that his place of residence offers no protection from immiseration and despair; in fact, it aggravates his life. When Raphael, the angel of the Lord disguised as a kinsman named Azariah, meets Tobit with joyful greetings, Tobit in his reply views his blindness as tantamount to death (5:10). Tobit's equation of blindness and death surely accords with the biblical belief that death is not necessarily non-existence but a most debilitating form of illness.[33] Therefore, to ask for the definitive face of death in prayer is hardly startling.

Sarah's loss of an honorable reputation and her utter failure to find a husband are a deathly sentence. Like Tobit, Sarah is also living as if dead.[34] In this regard, the prayers of Tobit and Sarah merely ask God to make their unique glimpses into death through their misfortunes an abiding reality. If death hovers over and defines their lives, Tobit and Sarah find no cause for continued existence. Like Job (cf. Job 3:1–26), Tobit and Sarah are alive but destroyed.

In their prayers, both Tobit and Sarah ask God to "release" them from a life of distress, pain, and shame. Tobit prays for God to allow him to go

31. Levenson, *Resurrection and the Restoration of Israel*, 172, 212.

32. Bailey, *Biblical Perspectives on Death*, 40.

33. See Levenson, *Resurrection and the Restoration of Israel*, 172. See also Tromp, *Primitive Conceptions of Death*, 212.

34. Ego ("The Book of Tobit and the Diaspora," 51) comments: "Asmodeus' relationship to Sarah causes death and barrenness." Of course, the story does not indicate whether Sarah is barren or not, only that she has had seven dead husbands.

into his eternal abode, which is often taken to mean the grave (3:6).[35] Sarah, on the other hand, asks God to release her from the earth but later asks God to have mercy on her (3:15 GI). Ironically, the God of the living responds by sending Raphael to "release" the cataracts from Tobit's eyes (3:17) and to "loose" the demon who has bound himself to Sarah. From God's point of view, "release" means life. For Tobit and Sarah, physical death is imagined as a release or a relief; what they both ask for is simply the ultimate or decisive expression of their experiences of the power of death in its various guises. Their prayers are laments that articulate their disorientation; their troubles point out that something is amiss in their relationship with God. And so, to request to be released into the eternal abode of the dead is to finalize their experience of God's absence.

The prayers of Tobit and Sarah express and respond to experiences of death in life, similar to what the psalmist gives voice to in Psalm 143.[36] Psalm 88:3–6 could very well be on Tobit's lips:

> For my soul is full of troubles, my life draws near to Sheol, I am counted among those who go down to the pit; I am like those who have no help, like those forsaken among the dead. Like the slain that lie in the grave, like those whom you remember no more, for they are cut off from your hand. You have put me in the depths of the Pit, in the regions dark and deep.

When Tobit tells Raphael that he does not have the light of heaven (5:10), he also echoes the psalmist in Psalm 13 who asks God to give light to his eyes lest he sleeps the sleep of death (Ps. 13:3–4). In the Book of Lamentations, the individual, in fact, expresses his experience of exile and devastation in language that recalls and can easily apply to the unfortunate experiences of Tobit and Sarah in exile. The individual describes his plight as walking in darkness, not in light, as being enveloped with bitterness and tribulation, and as sitting in the darkness like the dead of long ago (cf. Lam 3:1–6).

In many of the psalms, death is imagined as Sheol or the netherworld, as a place of darkness and shades, as the pit, or as the abode of the dead, bereft of God's presence. To go down to Sheol, which is the abyss or the lowest place, is not only to be most distant from the living God who lives

---

35. Beyerle ("Release Me," 76–82) surveys various texts that refer to "everlasting place" and notes that the expression cannot be simply identified with the grave since it can also connote death, Hades, and even heaven or the angelic sphere.

36. Nicklas ("Lesespaziergänge vom Buch Tobit," 66–73) makes a case from a reader-oriented approach for the interrelatedness of Tobit and the Psalms.

in the highest heavens (Ps 139:8) but also to be cut off from the land of the living and the closeness of kith and kin.[37] To go down to Sheol is to experience "the miserable conditions of diminished life" for it is "furnished with negative experiences, opposed to the favorable ones on earth and corresponding to the griefs of this life."[38] In other words, death is defined as a mode of being, an existence that is severed from the living God (Ps 88:4–7). God is, of course, the source of life and blessing. Praise is thus the response to the experience of divine blessings while lament is the response to experiences of death in life. Experiences of affliction identified in laments include loneliness and alienation (cf. Ps 38:12), mockery and verbal abuse (Ps 22:8), sickness (Ps 6:3), old age (Ps 71:9), and maltreatment by others (Ps 7:2). These are, of course, conditions that similarly destroy the lives of Tobit and Sarah. These manifestations of death can usher life back to dust. The prayers of Tobit and Sarah are, therefore, very similar to the laments in the psalms where images of death dominate. If indeed "the biblical Sheol is the prolongation of the unfulfilled life,"[39] then exile is like Sheol that prevents Tobit and Sarah from having a fulfilled and satisfied life. Tobit's hymn of praise in Tob 13:2, however, echoes the theme of God who raises people from the netherworld which is also typical in the psalms (cf. Ps 16:10; 30:4). Indeed, it is not outside God's power to save those whom he blesses from gloom and death. That Tobit and Sarah praise God's righteous qualities before they express their lament speaks to their confidence in God's deliverance (3:2, 11).[40]

Into this rotten world where darkness and death have a powerful hold on its inhabitants comes Tobiah, the son of Tobit. Hannah and Tobit call their son the "light of their eyes." Indeed, Tobiah will soon bring light upon their gloomy and shadowy universe. As a response to his prayer, God has Tobit's cataracts removed so that "he may see again God's sunlight" (3:17). Later, when Raphael reprises his instructions to Tobiah to cure his father's blindness, Raphael tells him to peel the white scales off his father's eyes and, according to GI 11:8, "he will see you," but, according to GII, "he will see the light." These two readings come together when, after his eyes were

---

37. See Levenson, *Resurrection and the Restoration of Israel*, 63–64. He notes the tension that exists between the older idea of Sheol as the universal destination of all and "a bold and younger affirmation of the Lord as Savior," which underscores the claim that there are those who die blessed like Abraham, Moses, and Job (75).

38. Tromp, *Primitive Conceptions of Death*, 212.

39. Levenson, *Resurrection and the Restoration of Israel*, 78.

40. See Frey-Anthes, "Praise," 149.

opened, Tobit exclaims, "I can see you son, the light of my eyes."[41] Under the guidance of the divine hand, Tobiah becomes a heroic figure, in fact a goʾel, who helps restore Tobit and Sarah into light and life. The return of Tobit's sight, of course, harks back to Isaiah's prophecy regarding the completion of Israel's suffering and the beginning of God's restorative act (cf. Isa 29:17–21). Often associated with exile, blindness is an illness that God will heal in the eschatological age. The liberation of Sarah from the tyranny of Asmodeus may also allude to Isa 49:24-25, where the promise to the exiles includes deliverance of those who have fallen prey to the tyrant.

THE PATH OF LIFE AND TRAINING IN RIGHTEOUSNESS

Tobit has done well with his wealth while serving as a purchasing agent for the king. Upon remembering the sum of money deposited with a cousin in Ecbatana, Tobit entrusts his son with the mission of retrieving it. The money will secure the welfare of his wife and son in the event of his death, which he expects to come soon. Before sending his son on a perilous journey, Tobit trains his son Tobiah with a series of instructions on righteousness, charity, and fidelity to the ways of God. Despite the ordeals that seem to invalidate the core of his beliefs, Tobit does not hesitate to hand these instructions on to his son. In his discourse, Tobit brings to the surface the principles that he learned from his grandmother Deborah and the values that have molded his life (1:8). Given at the nadir of his life, Tobit's discourse reveals the true test of his character and commitment.

From the beginning of the story, Tobit takes pride in his observance of the ways of righteousness and truth all the days of his life. Tobit lives the first part of his life in the land, and there he shows his mindfulness of God by fulfilling his Torah and ritual obligations. Despite being a member of a tribe from the north, Tobit goes to Jerusalem to worship at the Temple (1:6; 5:14).[42] In the later part of his life lived out in exile, Tobit remembers God by observing a kosher diet and refraining from eating the food of Gentiles (Tob 1:11), thus showing his resistance to assimilation to pagan culture. His acts of charity in the days of Shalmaneser while in exile also reveal his

41. See Macatangay, "Character Construction of Tobiah," 75–86.

42. Tobit claims that he goes alone in 1:6 but in 5:14, he claims that Hananiah and Nathan used to go with him to Jerusalem and were not led astray. Oeming ("Jewish Identity," 550) notes that the fact that Tobit goes alone "emphasizes the rebellion of the northern tribes, against which he stands as a solitary light."

remembrance of God. To celebrate the Feast of Pentecost, Tobit sends his son Tobiah with an invitation to bring in any poor person from his fellow co-religionists who are mindful of God (GI: "who is mindful of God," GII: "who is wholeheartedly mindful of God") to share a lavish meal with him (Tob 2:2).

But how likely is it for Tobiah to find in the streets of Nineveh a poor person who is truly mindful of God unless he knows the behaviors that define the parameters or the boundaries of what it means to walk in righteousness and in truth? Tobit certainly knows, as his own account declares. But can his young son tell? Identifying on the spot a poor person who is known for remembering God poses a difficult challenge for a young lad unless he recognizes certain concrete behaviors that divulge as much. In fact, all that the young boy could do, upon seeing one of their own people murdered, lying strangled out in the marketplace, was report the incident to his father, moving Tobit to leave his dinner behind in order to bury the dead, which the narrative considers as the poorest of the poor. As a member of the minority group, Tobit would likely know his fellow righteous Jews.

It is perhaps a narrative necessity then that before sending Tobiah on a dangerous journey Tobit should precisely instruct his son on what mindfulness of God entails. As a father who is aware of his responsibility to train his son in the faith of his fathers, Tobit must have felt that the time had come and so began his discourse by exhorting his son to remember or to keep the Lord in mind always. With his death a possibility and with his son's journey in view, Tobit offers his instructions for the way; they function as a paradigm for a lifestyle of remembering. And so, Tobit clarifies and specifies what being mindful of the Lord actually means. Identifying concrete behaviors that fall under his general instruction, Tobit tells Tobiah to honor his mother, to bury him and his wife properly in one grave upon their death, to marry a woman from his own ancestral family, to pay the wages of a worker on time, to seek the counsel of the wise, to bless the Lord, among others (Tob 4:3–21). Most importantly, however, Tobit urges Tobiah to lend financial aid to the poor and to perform acts of charity in order to show his remembrance of God. In fact, Tobit seems to equate the giving of alms with the practice of righteousness. Now equipped with these concrete instances of what it means to be mindful of God, Tobiah has some parameters to work with in discerning a sincere worshipper of God when he sees one.

The discourse of Tobit reminds Tobiah that if he walks on the path of righteousness and truth, he will be guided well and led along a good path (Tob 4:4–6, 19). As a type of wisdom figure, Tobit teaches his son in the ways that lead to life instead of death. Immediately after the scenes that describe Tobit's burial of the dead (2:1–8), Tobit's blindness (2:9–14), and his plea for God to send him to his everlasting home (3:1–6), which are all episodes that refer to or evoke death in the story, Tobit alludes to the possibility of life in his discourse (cf. 4:6, 10, 21). And now, having been instructed in the ways of the Lord, Tobiah embodies light and life, fully prepared to fulfill with success the mission his father Tobit has given him.[43] Indeed, the journey that Tobiah undertakes will restore the characters to life.

Raphael, who is the incarnation of divine providence in the story, accompanies and guides Tobiah on the journey to Ecbatana. Tobiah's dog follows them along (6:2). While walking along the river, a giant fish leaps out and almost devours the feet of Tobiah. Raphael instructs the young boy to seize the fish and to haul it on to the riverbank. He also tells Tobiah to slit the fish open and to take the gall, the heart, and the liver out for their therapeutic properties. Tobiah learns that the gall, when applied to the eyes of anyone with white scales, will restore the person's eyesight. He also learns from Raphael that the smoky stench produced from placing the heart and the liver upon live coals will cause the demon afflicting any individual to flee, leaving the person free from demonic control. And who would not flee from such a putrid and offensive smell? More importantly, Tobiah learns that he is the closest kin to Sarah, which means that he enjoys the right to marry her. Having heard of Sarah's plight, the new information predictably perturbs the young man, afraid that if he were to die, he would bring the life of his parents down to their grave in sorrow because there would be no one to give them a proper burial. Raphael reminds the young boy of his father's instruction to marry a kinswoman and teaches him what he needs to do in order to ward off the jealous demon from the bedroom.

Tobiah indeed marries Sarah, reversing her previous destiny from widowhood to wifehood, from singlehood to motherhood, and from ridicule to praise. After recovering the money, Tobit returns home with half of his father-in-law's property in tow, proving that God has made him prosperous and successful along the way. He removes the white blinding

---

43. On the role of Tobit's instructions in the narrative, see Macatangay, *Wisdom Instructions*, 139–66.

cataracts from his father's eyes, healing his blindness, a condition that earlier only worsened from consulting doctors (2:10). Tobiah's actions, deriving from his docile attention to the wise counsels of both Raphael and his father, have brought life to Sarah and Tobit who both previously prayed for death. Instead of being delivered into the darkness of the abyss, they receive light. Tobit, of course, finds out from the angelic revelation in the end that it is God who provides providential care to all those who remain faithful to him. Tobit's righteous acts demonstrating that he maintains a relationship with his God are not in vain in the land of his exile.

The eventual restoration of the lost son signifies life for Tobit and Hannah. Tobit's earlier mention in the story that his wife and his son were restored to him upon his nephew Ahiqar's intervention on his behalf after Esarhaddon became king (1:22; 2:1) anticipates the definitive restoration of the family upon Tobiah's return and marriage. Later, a parallel intervention that leads to the restoration of his son would be of a divine nature in the persona of Raphael. The wondrous angelic involvement averts the disaster of the monstrous fish and the death-dealing demon that could have easily rendered Tobiah lifeless.[44] God's providential care shown in the miracle-laden journey that culminates in the marriage of Tobiah and Sarah has ensured the preservation of the continuity and integrity of the family of Tobit. When Raphael tells Tobiah not to be afraid of the marriage because Sarah has been set apart for him and mentions that Tobiah "will have children by her who will take the place of brothers" (5:18), the marriage looks forward to the restoration, preservation, and fecundity of the family line. Raphael's earlier suggestion of children in this marriage is evident as well in the nuptial prayer in which Tobiah claims that "the human race descended" from Adam and Eve, suggesting "his hope for children."[45] In other words, the return of the presumed lost child and the marriage of the son bode well for the family of Tobit. All of these happen because God, in his angel Raphael, shows his power to reverse the life-threatening adversity, restoring Tobit and his family to life. A situation of death leads to enrichment and the restoration of the family because of God's providential intervention. Since the story of Tobit has a national focus as well, conjoining personal and collective redemption, it is reasonable to say that it is by divine providence that Israel lives. If Tobit's story is true, then it hints at the possibility that Israel's

44. In GI, the fish tried to devour the boy. In GII, the fish tried to swallow the foot of the boy.

45. Nowell, "An Ancestral Story," 12.

misfortunes—the humiliations of exile, defeat, ridicule—are temporary states of affairs that will soon come to an end.

As the story closes, Tobit praises God and expresses the hopes that God will restore the household of Israel to its glory just as God has done for him and his household. At the summing up of life and before he sleeps the sleep of the just, Tobit gives a farewell discourse to his household, instructing Tobiah and his children to practice righteousness and charity. He cites the example of his nephew Ahiqar to illustrate the saving worth of charity. He also predicts the destruction of Nineveh, telling his son to leave the city. Tobiah buries his father in the same grave as his mother, thereby showing his obedience to his father's command to grant them a proper burial after their deaths. Tobiah lived in prosperity and died highly respected.

This note seems to conclude the narrative. Still, that Tobiah lives in Media is a stark reminder that the descendants of Tobit live far away from the land. The experience of divine help, however, allows Tobit and his family to look forward to the hopes that history and the divine promise will meet at "the appointed times" (14:4). When God radically enacts his mercy on behalf of the faithful remnants, Tobit's descendants will be restored to the land and to life.

In the last scenes of the story, the mention of Tobit's grandchildren balances the picture of exile; a pointer to life counters the situation of death. In addition to the claim that Tobit died in peace, old and full of days, Tobit receives an honorable burial. These are all signs of a blessed and completed life. Moreover, like Abraham, Jacob, and Joseph, Tobit dies fulfilled with a full view of his future lineage (14:3). After immersion into the darkness, the divine blessing of progeny is realized and the threat of non-existence vanishes. That life has the final word in a worldview that prizes the perpetuation of the family line and name is highly meaningful. The conclusion of the story portrays Tobit as a righteous individual in whom God's blessings are actualized and fulfilled. Of course, the signs of life and blessings in the midst of exile and death can be taken as a likely indication that the divine promise of land continues to take hold. If the covenant promises of blessing and progeny are fulfilled in Tobit's life, then the other covenant promise of inheritance is likely to come true as well. For what is the promise of a full life other than life lived in the land!

CONCLUDING REMARKS

The Book of Tobit is ultimately a narrative of the Diaspora viewed through the eyes of exile. Exile is no longer an event but a metaphor for the Diaspora experience. In the misfortunes of Tobit and Sarah, the effects of exile become an experience that is particular and concrete. Their individually narrated afflictions, shame, and vulnerabilities point to the greater adversity of exile; alienation from the land is refracted through their individual troubles and tragedies. As an experience of disintegration and dissipation, the absence of a homeland is a pointer to darkness and death. Might this be one reason why the narrative is so preoccupied with the burial of the dead?

Exile and death are not necessarily the last word in the story of Tobit's family and the household of God. Tobit has experienced the abyss in exile, a realm thought to be the farthest from God, bereft of divine care and remembrance. And yet, Tobit has also experienced the presence and nearness of God's providence, providing him the sure and certain hope that God can stave off the forces of death and bring him back to life. What Tobit has experienced, Israel can await. As is true of Tobit's family (11:17), joy will resound again in the household of Jacob. In the meantime, almsgiving and other acts of charity are ways to maintain a proper and righteous relationship with the God of life. Acts of charity in the dispersion are ways to stir God into remembrance of his covenant with his people. And so, it is only fitting to investigate the many claims that Tobit makes on behalf of almsgiving and charity.

2

ALMSGIVING AND ACTS OF CHARITY IN THE BOOK OF TOBIT

THE BOOK OF TOBIT is the only book in the Septuagint and the Christian Bible that makes acts of charity central to its narrative.[1] As the story begins, Tobit states that he worshipped at the Temple as long as it was possible and declares that he performed in the land of his exile many charitable works for his people who had been deported with him (1:3). Immediately after describing the many exemplary acts of Temple-related piety such as tithing, pilgrimages, sacrificial offerings, and calendric observances that he accomplished while in the land, Tobit once again insists on his acts of charity. They include giving bread to the hungry, clothing the naked, and burying the dead (1:16–18).

The story further identifies behavior that illustrates Tobit to be a dedicated almsgiver. Despite his reduced means after losing his source of income from the royal court, Tobit still desires to feed his poor co-religionists who are mindful of God with a festive meal to celebrate Pentecost. Despite the king's decree against it, despite his neighbors' mockery, and despite the threat of contamination and ritual impurity, Tobit still continues to bury the dead. The risk to his life and freedom and the constraints on his resources have not stopped Tobit from performing acts of charity. Burdensome though the costs may be, Tobit does not blink an eye when it comes to charitable works. If anything at all, he is persistent in doing charity no

---

1. The Greek word *eleēmosynē*, which is preponderant in the Book of Tobit, is often translated as charity, mercy, and almsgiving.

matter what it may entail.[2] Tobit is truly a fool for charity. No wonder then that in a discourse before entrusting Tobiah with a mission to retrieve a sum of money deposited with a cousin, Tobit asks his son to engage in acts of charity by giving alms out of his abundance, by giving food to the hungry, and by clothing the naked (4:7–11, 16–17). His instructions, in fact, seem to reduce his general command to remember the Lord and to practice righteousness to charity and almsgiving to *personae miserae*.

After becoming blind, Tobit notes that all his kinsmen grieved at his condition (2:10). He underscores, however, the benevolent care that his nephew Ahiqar extended to him in a time of dire need. In fact, the verb that Tobit employs to describe Ahiqar's care for him connotes the supply of the necessary nourishment and provision for Tobit's physical needs for a considerable period of time. The verb used to denote the action of Ahiqar captures Tobit's complete dependence and fragility since it "paints the image of one man feeding the other like a child."[3] As he addresses his son and grandchildren with a final will and testament on his deathbed at the end of the story, Tobit cites the example of almsgiving that Ahiqar gave him. He points out that Ahiqar's act of kindness towards him prevented Ahiqar from falling into a dark and deadly trap that his nephew Nadab had set for him. He mentions Ahiqar's compassionate care to drive home an important lesson about the power of almsgiving to deliver from death.

Raphael also gives a discourse as he reveals to Tobit and Tobiah the whole truth behind the course of events in the story. In his speech, Raphael points out that "it is better to give alms than to store up gold" (12:8b). Raphael, in fact, presented a memorial of Tobit's prayer and act of charity before the throne of the Most High, moving God to charge the angel to heal Tobit's blindness (12:11–14). Emphasizing the salvific power of almsgiving in his speech, Raphael practically confers divine approval upon Tobit's claims regarding charity.[4]

In his discourse to his son, Tobit provides a number of reasons why the performance of charity and almsgiving is deemed important. The first motivation Tobit provides for why Tobiah is to engage in almsgiving is that it merits a similar action on God's part. God will not turn his face away

---

2. Weeks ("Deuteronomic Heritage," 393) underlines the negative aspect of Tobit's almsgiving: "Tobit is a pious man, to be sure, but his piety comes close to the point of being obsessive and self-destructive, while his sense of isolated righteousness neglects the price paid by others for his behavior."

3. Portier-Young, "Alleviation of Suffering," 41.

4. See Macatangay, *Wisdom Instructions*, 169–71.

from anyone who does not turn his or her face away from the poor (4:7). Tobit also claims that giving in proportion to the gifts received or from whatever little one has is a way to store up a good treasure for oneself against the day of necessity (4:8–9). Tobit further claims that almsgiving delivers from death and the darkness (4:10). Tobit drives home this particular lesson about almsgiving when he cites the example of his nephew Ahiqar in his farewell discourse (14:11). Finally, Tobit declares that almsgiving is an excellent offering before God (4:11).

In his exhortation before ascending to heaven, Raphael also acknowledges the purchasing power of almsgiving. After urging Tobit and Tobiah to acknowledge always the deeds of God, Raphael assures them that almsgiving is better than both prayer and fasting and that it is better to give alms than to store up gold (4:8–9). He provides three reasons why almsgiving is the better way: 1) it saves from death, 2) it purges away all sin, and 3) it leads to an enjoyment of a full life (12:8–10).

If one compares the reasons for almsgiving that Tobit and Raphael provide in their respective discourses, they both assert that almsgiving has the power to save the almsgiver from death and darkness. It is equally likely that they both see almsgiving to have a redemptive value. Raphael categorically asserts it while Tobit's claim regarding almsgiving as a worthy sacrifice before God may be an oblique way to refer to the salvific value of almsgiving. One reason for almsgiving that the angel provides but which Tobit does not explicitly state is the claim that almsgiving leads to an enjoyment of a full life. Perhaps, only an angel of God can make a promise of life on behalf of God. Certainly, the narrative resolution that shows Tobit the avid almsgiver with restored eyesight, a doubly enriched son, and a full lineage in view at his deathbed proves the angelic statement that almsgiving leads to a satisfied and abundant life. And so, Tobit's claim that almsgiving keeps one from going into the dark abode functions as the equivalent of Raphael's claim regarding the life-satisfying value of almsgiving.

With the seemingly incessant references to works of charity and almsgiving, the Book of Tobit can be described as a fitting dramatization and endorsement of Tobit's tenets regarding the value of almsgiving. In Tobit's worldview, charity takes the pride of place because it confers a multitude of benefits. Therefore, in this chapter, it is essential to review in more detail the claims that the story makes regarding acts of charity.

ALMSGIVING AND THE JOURNEY OF TOBIAH

After his prayer asking God to send him to his everlasting home, Tobit believes that his death looms on the horizon. Tobit calls his son Tobiah to inform him about a sum of money that he previously entrusted to Gabael, a cousin who resides at Rages in Media (5:2; 9:6). Before sending him, Tobit instructs his son in the ways of righteousness and truth, specifically commanding him to give alms and to perform charity (4:4–11). Despite glaring evidence to the contrary, Tobit holds firm to his belief regarding almsgiving. As an ardent practitioner of almsgiving, Tobit wants his son to continue in the same vein. As the story later reveals, it is Tobit's commitment to almsgiving that is in fact the subject of his testing.[5]

Tobit is well aware that the roads to Media are unsafe. Tobit himself admits that he is afraid to go there (1:15). That he asks his son to look for a traveling companion is an acknowledgment of the great risks that the journey poses to his son's life. The worries that Hannah expresses to Tobit speak to the possibility that Tobiah might never return home; in a retort, she implies that sending Tobiah away is sending him to his death (5:18–19). After all, travel in those days is a risky enterprise and a true adventure the end of which is never known.[6] Indeed, the story develops the journey of Tobiah with menace and danger constantly lurking on the horizon, with a fish anxious to devour him and a demon ready to kill him. The night setting renders the journey with an ill-omened ambiance (cf. 6:2).[7] By sending him on this journey, Tobit is risking the life of his only son, the staff of his hands in old age.

Why is Tobit willing to risk everything including his son? Tobit's emphasis on and commitment to almsgiving is one possible reason why he takes the chance and forsakes the danger to his own son's life. His specific instructions on performing charity and the giving of alms as a way of

5. See Anderson, *Charity*, 85–88.

6. See Vilchez, *Tobiah y Judit*, 41. On the dangers and hardships of ancient travel, see Casson, *Travel in the Ancient World*, 72–76.

7. Nowell, *Narrative Technique*, 220, notes that, while the word for day dominates the first and last section of the story, the Greek word for night characterizes the travels of Tobiah, the middle section of the narrative. Fields, "The Motif of Night as Danger," 22, observes that "deep darkness—צלמות—is a metaphor for things evil and feared, not for things that are good and loved. For the ancient reader the evening/night setting would almost certainly have imbued each narrative from the outset with an aura of foreboding and sinister premonition, of trepidation and anxiety, for night and violence, danger and darkness were inseparably joined."

remembering God suggests that Tobit wants his son to take on the role of a generous almsgiver. Since Tobit has become poor and is no longer in any position to give alms, the surest way for Tobiah to become an almsgiver rather than an impecunious alms receiver after Tobit's death is to happen upon a substantial sum of money.[8] The retrieval of the deposited pouches containing a great sum of money would allow Tobiah to continue in his father's stead and practice.

The motif of remembering occurs five times in the fourth chapter thus creating the impression that the chapter is built around the idea of remembrance. The notion of remembering plays, in fact, a vital role in linking Tobit's discourse and Tobiah's journey. The theological and practical realities that arise from the act of remembering intersect here. Tobit's remembrance of the money necessitates the risky journey of Tobiah while Tobit's command to remember the Lord has to translate into the practice of charity. To a great extent, Tobit's instructions and Tobiah's perilous journey are closely connected in that they have a common lofty end in view: to place Tobiah in a position of almsgiver. The journey and the instructions both contribute to the shaping of the character and identity of Tobiah.

Taking up the bulk of Tobit's discourse, the particular instructions on almsgiving and the mission to recover the money are ways to equip Tobiah for almsgiving and to mold him in his father's image and likeness. These are the necessary conditions that will transform the son into a living copy of his father. When the instructions are received and the sum of money is retrieved, Tobit the almsgiver will continue to live on in his son not only in the physical sense of blood and name but also in a moral sense.[9] With virtually identical names, Tobit's identity survives, reappears, and continues in an offspring who acts as he did.[10] One could almost hear in Tobit's words to his son a distant echo of the well known song "all of me, why not take all of me."

---

8. Anderson, *Charity*, 89–90; Anderson, "Does Tobit Fear God," 123. See also Di Pede, *Reveler*, 45.

9. See Priero, *Tobiah*, 77. The idea is also echoed in Sir 30:2–5. See also Crenshaw, *Education in Ancient Israel*, 3.

10. Levenson, *Resurrection and the Restoration of Israel*, 109–10, discusses the importance of the idea of the survival of identity in a kin or descendant for making sense of Ezekiel's vision of David's appointment as the shepherd over Israel, "for David's identity was not restricted to the one man of that name but can reappear to a large measure in kin who share it" (110).

ALMSGIVING AS AN ACT OF SOLIDARITY

In theory, the Temple offers a system of assistance and provision for the poor, the widow, and the orphan from the tithes offered for their sake. Deut 14:28–29 and 26:12 stipulate that the tithes on the produce of the third year are to be given to those who do not possess land: the Levite, the alien, the poor, and the widow, so that they can eat their fill in the community. In the absence of the temple, the structure for the care of the marginalized is not in place. The situation in Tobit's Diaspora must have been comparable, with the poor kin of Tobit having no recourse for help. That Tobit seeks out and invites the righteous poor to celebrate Pentecost with a meal points to this possibility. In this case, to give as alms to the righteous poor the money meant as tithes for the Temple, as Tobit envisions, has the social function of helping the poor and the least in the Diaspora; they are, after all, strangers in a foreign land. Almsgiving and other acts of charity are viewed as a form of mutual and communal support. For without them, life in the Diaspora could be a jungle.

Having lost the ground beneath his feet, Tobit reconstructs something to stand on by way of social affinities. Every character in the narrative is related to another, with the term "brother" or "sister" occurring with such high frequency in the story that the "network of relations among these characters creates an extended family that threatens to take over all of Assyria."[11] The social affinities of family and kinship have become the source of constancy and stability in a state of exile.[12] To this end, the practice of giving alms integrates and unites the dispersed members of the household of Israel. It fosters internal cohesion in the community and it preserves the bonds of kinship. Mutual assistance reinforces common ties in the dispersion.[13] In short, works of charity assist the materially destitute, build up the community, and enhance solidarity among kin.[14] Such social significance and value of almsgiving may have served as motive for why

11. Wills, *The Jewish Novel*, 78

12. On kinship in Tobit, see Skemp, "Theme of Kinship," 92–103; see also Dimant, "The Family of Tobit," 157–62.

13. See for instance, Otzen, *Tobit and Judith*, 35–37; Moore, *Tobit*, 176; Rabenau, *Studien zum Buch* Tobit, 132–34.

14. See Deselaers, *Buch Tobit*, 351–54. Craghan (*Esther, Judith, Tobit*, 134) notes that the stress on almsgiving is a show of concern for fellow Jews in which "Jewish commitment to God is measured by Jewish commitment to the community of God."

Tobit commands his son to restrict his practice of almsgiving to fellow Israelites (2:2; 4:6).[15]

The compassionate care that Ahiqar extends to his uncle Tobit in a period of great distress (1:22; 2:10) is a prime example of almsgiving as an act of solidarity. A non-Israelite figure popularly known for his wise counsels, the story ignores Ahiqar's pagan wisdom and portrays him instead as a nephew celebrated for his charity.[16] In his farewell discourse, Tobit sets Ahiqar up as a paragon of almsgiving (cf. Tob 14:11). Ahiqar's charity matters more than his sagacity. Ahiqar fits the familial network of Tobit by virtue of his benevolent care; his almsgiving is the essence of belonging to Tobit's household. Since the figure of Ahiqar is remembered in the narrative for his charity, his example shows that the practice of almsgiving opens up the tight communal structure and facilitates the incorporation of non-Israelites within the household of Israel.[17] Charity has come to define what it means to be in solidarity with God's people.

Finally, almsgiving as a form of assistance helps ensure the survival of kin and the extended household. Acts of charity can certainly contribute to the continuation of Tobit's ancestral line after his death if descendants survive. Almsgiving is a form of assistance by and to the members of the household of Israel with the goal of safeguarding the continuity and preservation of the family lineage. Since identity and felicity are firmly embedded within the family, the avoidance of family extinction is a matter of prime importance. Acts of charity are meant to ensure the survival of a remnant (cf. 13:16). In this way, acts of charity are acts of solidarity with the dead

---

15. Fitzmyer, *Tobit*, 169, claims that Tobit's advice "speaks of respect being had among those who pursue righteousness."

16. According to Fitzmyer, *Tobit*, 32, "there is good reason to consider Ahiqar a historical person and a Gentile, but to imply that he was son of a Jewish ἀδελφός goes too far." Fitzmyer, *Tobit*, 334, notes that Nadin, the villain in the story of Ahiqar, "epitomizes what's wrong with Nineveh." Following this suggestion, Kottsieper, "'Look Son, What Nadab Did to Ahikaros,'" 149, 159, 161, maintains that the story is not meant to provide another example to support the book's doctrine that righteousness saves. Rather, it is meant to illustrate the treachery or wickedness of Nineveh, which can influence persons like Nadin, the nephew of Ahiqar, to act wickedly, bringing righteous people such as his uncle Ahiqar into great peril.

17. See Weigl, "Die rettende Macht der Barmherzigkeit," 212–43. See also Zappella, *Tobit,* 22–24. Tobit's universalistic vision of the earth's inhabitants ascending Jerusalem with gifts in their hands to worship the God of Israel in Tob 13:11 recalls the prophetic claims regarding the nations (cf. Isa 2:2; Mic 4:1–2; Zech 8:21–22).

and the living done for the sake of the common pursuit of preserving the household.

ALMSGIVING AS AN ACT OF REMEMBRANCE

Aside from social and humanitarian values, almsgiving has a strong theological function. To offer material kindness to the poor is to remember God. In the Diaspora, acts of charity are acts of remembering God. Tobit notes that while in exile, his remembrance of God shows in abstaining from eating Gentile food (1:11). Since Tobit mentions his performance of charitable works such as feeding the hungry, clothing the naked, and burying the dead immediately after referring to his dietary observance, they presumably reveal likewise his mindfulness of God. In the Diaspora, his almsgiving and other acts of charity have become substitutes for his pious observance of the divine commands. In fact, the two parallel statements with which Tobit starts his discourse show that performing good works is remembering God. Tobit exhorts his son Tobiah:

> "Through all your days, son, remember the Lord our God and do not desire to sin or transgress his precepts."

> "Perform righteousness all the days of your life and do not walk on the paths of unrighteousness." (4:5)

These parallel instructions both have an admonition and a prohibition. The positive exhortations are to remember the Lord and to perform righteousness. "Do not transgress God's commands" and "do not walk on the paths of wrongdoing" are the negative injunctions. Tobit's general instruction reflects the idiom of the two ways in sorting out the wise from the foolish typical of sapiential literature. The antithetical sentence structure instills the lesson that the wise/righteous will succeed but the foolish/wicked will perish. In this case, if Tobiah remembers the Lord and performs righteousness, he will walk on the path of wisdom. On the other hand, if he transgresses God's commands, he is on the road of foolishness. The parallelism reveals that to remember the Lord is to perform righteousness and to transgress God's commands is to walk on the path of wrongdoing.[18] Remembrance is observance of the Lord's precepts.

---

18. See Macatangay, "Acts of Charity," 69–84.

Tobit specifies and clarifies what it means to perform righteousness. He instructs Tobiah to do acts of charity by engaging in almsgiving to the poverty-stricken, by giving to the hungry some of his food, and by clothing the naked; he is not to turn his face away from the poor (4:7–8, 16). Tobit's instruction makes clear that acts of charity have become the practical equivalent of practicing righteousness. In the short Greek version of Tob 4:10, in fact, Tobit claims that almsgiving saves while in Tob 14:11, Tobit says that righteousness saves. This is another clear indication that the story views righteousness and almsgiving to be interchangeable, if not synonymous. Being righteous means more than proper behavior; to be righteous is to observe the law, which for Tobit, means to engage personally in charitable acts that benefit the poor.

Dan 4:24 makes a similar claim—to be righteous is to extend material kindness to the downtrodden. After Nebuchadnezzar's fateful dream about a gigantic tree that is cut down, the parallelism of the structure in Daniel's advice to the king to redeem his sins by good deeds and to be generous to the poor bears this out.[19] Thus, benevolent activities towards the poor manifest and concretize righteousness such that to perform righteousness is to do works for *personae miserae* that arise from a profound sense of mercy.

For Tobit, to remember God implies the concrete and practical acts of mercy just as his command to Tobiah to remember the sorrows of his mother entails the practical task of caring for her in widowhood and old age (4:4). In this way, the very tangible action of extending charity to the poor is not only an act of righteousness but also an act that points to faith in and remembrance of God. Indeed, acts of mercy convey a social function in which cohesion and solidarity of the members of the community are fostered. Primarily though, they are religious acts that express mindfulness of God. In later Hebrew and Aramaic textual traditions of the Book of Tobit and in rabbinic literature, the religious dimension of almsgiving and tithing become more pronounced, explicitly stating that almsgiving is a religious duty.[20]

Tobit's emphasis on almsgiving as an act of remembering God is a vital textual witness in Second Temple Judaism to the claim that the visible expression of the elect's relationship with God is not limited to the Temple

19. See Rosenthal, "Sedaka," 411–30; Anderson, *Sin*, 137–41; see also Rabenau, *Studien zum Buch Tobit*, 130–31; Zanella, "Between Righteousness and Alms," 269–87.

20. See Weeks et al., *Texts from the Principal Ancient and Medieval Traditions*, 39–46.

alone. The hands of the poor stretched out in supplication are as holy as the altar of sacrifice such that "placing coins in the hand of a beggar is like putting sacrifice on the altar—for both the hand and the altar provide direct access to God."[21] By emphasizing almsgiving as a religious duty that manifests mindfulness of God, Tobit defines service to God in horizontal and vertical terms. This does not mean, however, that acts of charity abrogates or replaces the Temple cult. As the story begins, Tobit juxtaposes the cultic and the charitable as he claims that he has walked in the path of truth and righteousness all his life. As the story ends, Tobit sings of his lively hopes for the restoration of the Jerusalem Temple, implying the continuing relevance and validity of ritual acts. What Tobit does is enfold acts of mercy into the cult and the Temple in which service at the altar is harmonized with service to the needy. The cultic and the charitable become two inseparable modes of rendering worship and service to God.

ALMSGIVING AS A WORTHY OFFERING

Tobit ties almsgiving to the ritual sacrifices of the Temple more clearly in his discourse. He tells Tobiah that almsgiving, for all those who practice it, is an excellent offering in the presence of God the Most High (4:11). Tobit here employs the concept of δῶρον, which normally has a cultic connotation. Found in Pentateuch texts like LXX Lev 1:2–3; 3:6–8 and Num 7:12–13, this term is a sacrificial terminology that refers to the offerings in the prescriptions for sacrifices. Tobit employs the term earlier in the narrative without any cultic color. In a response to Tobit's question regarding the source of the goat, Anna claims that the animal is a δῶρον given to her on top of her wages as a weaver (cf. GI Tob 2:14). As such, the term is not necessarily cultic but can simply suggest the profane sense of "a charitable gift" given to a person.[22] In Tobit's hymn of praise, however, Tobit predicts the rebuilding of Jerusalem and describes the exodus of many nations drawn to the name of God, bearing in their hands δῶρα or gifts for the King of Heaven (cf. Tob 13:13). Here and in Tobit's discourse, δῶρον is referred to God, conveying the vertical or cultic aspect of the term. In Tobit's discourse, the cultic overtone of the word is confirmed when he claims that alms are a way to make deposits into a goodly treasure. Almsgiving and sacrifice intersect,

---

21. Anderson, *Sin*, 148.

22. See Di Pede, *Reveler*, 45n56, who suggests that the term should be translated in the sense of a "charitable gift" given to others and one that favors the giver.

for alms as gifts before God function in the same way as sacrifices—they transport the goods to God.[23]

By relating almsgiving to δῶρον, Tobit does not invalidate cultic offerings; he merely expands the semantic range or content of this cultic concept to include works of charity. Alms to the needy, like cereal offerings, are acceptable gifts before God. Almsgiving and other works of charity are now equally valid offerings comparable to the ritual offerings in the Jerusalem Temple. By including alms as part of the cultic furniture, Tobit presupposes the religious duty to offer sacrifices. This further points to the strong likelihood that charity and cult have equal weight in terms of their redemptive efficacy.

Tobit's claim that almsgiving is an excellent gift before God finds approval and legitimacy in Raphael's revelation that a memorial of Tobit's prayer and act of charity was presented before the throne of God, moving God to commission his angel to heal him (12:11–14).[24] In Leviticus, a memorial has cultic resonances as it is related to the ritual act of presenting and burning on the altar part of the cereal offering which becomes a sweet-smelling oblation before God (cf. Lev 2:2). In Tobit's hands, the self-same memorial includes his act of burying the dead. The cultic language of memorial then imagines Tobit's prayer and act of charity as a pleasing and fragrant oblation that rises into the presence of God. Like the sacrifices on the altar in the Temple, Tobit's prayer and almsgiving bear him up before the throne of the Most High, stirring God to remember him.

In Raphael's disclosure of the whole truth, the gift of alms can also be viewed as part of the sacrificial reciprocity between Tobit and God. As alms are excellent gifts, Tobit offers to God alms in proportion to what he has and receives in return more than what he has offered. God gives the blessings of sight, prosperity, and a restored household to Tobit in exchange for his gifts of almsgiving and prayer. Of course, it is not much for God to grant these blessings. For Tobit, the charitable acts that he offers to God are costly; to give this little is to give much. And yet, God's recompense in exchange for Tobit's little is abundant life, all because almsgiving has become a worthy gift before God.[25]

23. Anderson, *Sin*, 165.

24. See Macatangay, *Wisdom Instructions*, 108; Ego, "Tobit's weisheitliches Vermächtniss," 95–122.

25. See Anderson, "Sacrifice," 872.

Since Tobit is in exile, Tobit can only instruct his son to engage in continual prayer and to bless God (4:19). He cannot exhort his son to perform the ritual obligations he once kept in the land. He is unable to instruct his son to present sacrifices in the Temple or to offer tithes to orphans and widows even in monetary form as the Mosaic Law prescribes (cf. Deut 14:22–28) and as he once did. He can only translate the pecuniary offerings to the Temple as alms and offer almsgiving and other acts of benevolence as actions that satisfy the sacrificial requirements of the cult. And so, Tobit adds an ethical and horizontal component into the ritual prescriptions regarding sacrifices, specifying acts of charity to be excellent gifts before the heavenly temple of God.

The narrative episode that describes Tobit's celebration of Pentecost also makes this clear. Pentecost, or the Feast of Weeks in celebration of the first fruits of the wheat harvest, is one of the three solemn Jewish feasts that all Jewish males are required to celebrate by making a pilgrimage to Jerusalem and by offering sacrifices (cf. Exod 34:22–23; Deut 16:16–17; cf. also Num 28:26). As a harvest feast, Jews on Pentecost are to present an offering of new grain and first fruits of the harvest to the Lord along with a burnt offering of seven unblemished first-year lambs, a bull, and two rams (Lev 23:15–21). In addition to the specific offerings on Pentecost, Leviticus further decrees that the gleanings of the harvest are to be left for the poor and the stranger (Lev 23:22). Of course, Tobit observes and celebrates this important feast of Pentecost in the Diaspora not by presenting such offerings but by feeding the poor with a festive meal and by burying the dead (2:1–5). Instructed by the law not to come empty-handed, Tobit's acts of charity fill his hands before the Lord on the Feast of Weeks; Tobit seems to consider them to be worthy offerings to God on the solemn feast of Pentecost.

ALMSGIVING AND SIN

In asserting that almsgiving is a worthy sacrifice, Tobit may also be implying that works of charity have some salvific value. When Tobit tells Tobiah that almsgiving delivers from death and keeps one from entering into the dark abode (4:10), he intimates that almsgiving and other acts of charity may be viewed as fulfilling the function of the atoning rituals of the temple.

The Book of Tobit is not quite precise in what death means or how to envision the afterlife.[26] As suggested earlier, however, death can be taken as

26. See Beyerle, "Release Me," 71–88.

a metaphor that vividly captures the experience of exile and the resultant debilitation and disintegration of the nation. It is likely that Tobit views death as a type of punishment for sin that may be expiated or escaped through acts of charity. Two episodes in the story hint at such a likelihood. First, in his prayer after becoming blind and desolate, Tobit seems to identify with the collective sins of his people. He implores God not to punish him for his sins or for his oversights or for the sins of his ancestors who disobeyed God for which they were given over to plunder, exile, and death (3:3–4).[27] The prayer creates the impression that death is a punishment for sin and disobedience of the divine commands. It clearly conforms to the biblical view of the diaspora as divine punishment for Israel's sins. Certainly, the story portrays Tobit as a righteous individual, one who has not committed any sins. And yet, because he is in exile along with those deported to Nineveh, Tobit feels implicated. If plunder, exile, and death are punishment for sin, then Tobit's exilic situation involves him in the collective guilt. With his blindness, Tobit identifies with wayward Israel. When his eyes are opened, he learns from Raphael that his prayer and charitable work of burying the dead have earned some redemptive worth before God. The angelic revelation shows that Tobit's escape from death and darkness is somehow linked to his benevolent deed. Second, the story of Ahiqar and Nadab in Tobit's farewell speech illustrates his point about the salvific value of almsgiving. Since Ahiqar had given alms, he escaped the trap of death while his nephew Nadab fell into the eternal darkness as a result of his sin, wickedness, and treachery.

The discourse of Raphael to Tobit and Tobiah in 12:8–10 underscores even more distinctly the efficacious power of almsgiving.

> Prayer with fasting is good, but better than both is almsgiving with righteousness. A little with righteousness is better than wealth with wrongdoing. It is better to give alms than to lay up gold. For almsgiving saves from death and purges away every sin.

The angelic speech endorses Tobit's earlier dictum, affirming the exceptional expiatory efficacy of almsgiving. As a sin remover, almsgiving beats the usual expressions of repentance such as prayer and fasting. Raphael could not have stated it more directly: almsgiving wipes out all sin and saves from death (12:9).[28] Since exile and death are the punishments for sin, efforts

27. Moore, *Tobit*, 32, claims that the author "makes it clear that Israel brought its painful exile upon itself (cf. 3:3–5; 13:3–6, 9)."

28. Other Second Temple texts express similar sentiments. In Dan 4:24, Daniel

need to be made to "purge" Israel of its sin and to pay off its debt. Tobit offers almsgiving as a way to clear the exiled community of its sin.

In his revelatory speech, Raphael uses ἀποκαθαίρω, a Greek verb which the *Greek-English Lexicon* defines as "to cleanse," "to clear," "to get rid of," or "to remove by purging or clearing."[29] The four times that the verb occurs in the Septuagint (Tob 12:9; Prov 15:27; Job 7:9; 9:30) do not refer to expiation of sin or atonement. Hence, the verb is usually taken to refer to mere moral cleansing or purgation rather than an act of atonement. Since Tob 12:9 underscores prayer, fasting, and almsgiving as ways to repent or "purge" every sin, with almsgiving given a more prominent role, the verse may indeed be saying that such acts of charity can deliver a person from the negative effects of sinful actions.[30] The immediate context, which refers to the power of almsgiving to save from death, may suggest "that the cleansing refers to a removal of guilt and punishment rather than mere moral transformation."[31] More precisely, when sin is understood or imagined as debt, the verb conveys a financial sense in terms of clearance or cancelation of an obligation. The meaning of the verb then would bend toward the notion of clearing instead of cleansing or purging. In this way, almsgiving and other acts of charity fund a proper treasury that can help cancel, clear, eliminate or pay off the debt accrued through sins.[32]

ALMSGIVING AND THE FULL LIFE

Raphael further informs Tobit and Tobiah that those who give alms shall enjoy a full life; they will be sated in life. Life here means the fullness of earthly life in the here and now, not in the afterlife.[33] The logic here seems to flow from Deuteronomy but with a slight twist. If indeed almsgiving is a concrete instance of remembering God and of observing the divine com-

---

advises the king to atone for his sins by good deeds. Sir 3:30 agrees with Tobit and Daniel, categorically stating that almsgiving propitiates sins while *2 Clem* 16:4, a later text, follows this teaching, asserting that almsgiving serves as atonement for sins and lightens the burden of sins.

29. Liddell and Scott, "ἀποκαθαίρω," 200.

30. See von Stemm, *Der betende Sünder vor Gott*, 179–80.

31. Quarles, "New Perspective and Atonement," 46.

32. Anderson ("How Does Almsgiving Purge Sins?," 1–14) traces the linguistic development of this understanding. See Anderson, *Sin*, 24–55.

33. Fitzmyer, *Tobit*, 293. See also Skemp, *Vulgate of Tobit*, 365–66.

mandments, and if to obey the commandments is to receive life and avoid death, it is not surprising that almsgiving would lead to life. Tobit, however, has to learn this lesson the hard way through a test. It is only retrospectively that the positive turn of events in Tobit's life proves that those who give alms are divinely rewarded with a blessed and full earthly existence. A full life, of course, is a life favored by God.

The discourses of Tobit and Raphael both stress almsgiving and righteousness. Between the instructions of Tobit in chapter 4 and the proverbial counsels of Raphael in chapter 12, however, the central section of the narrative refers neither to works of charity nor to righteousness. At first glance, the discourses, which serve as literary bookends, do not seem connected to the journey of Tobiah. And yet, the voyage of Tobiah details the events that will lead to his marriage to Sarah and the discovery of the cure for his father's blindness. To a great extent, the providential events in the adventures of Tobiah recounted in Tobit 5–11 are for the sake of Tobit the devoted almsgiver; the course of events has Tobit in special view. When his son returns, Tobit is cured of his blindness, his household is greatly enriched, and his family line continues. And so, although the themes of almsgiving and righteousness stressed in the discourses are nowhere referred to in the journey of Tobiah, the dramatization of the divinely directed adventure nonetheless indicates and affirms the claims of Tobit and Raphael regarding charity. Essentially, Tobit's risk-taking in the sending of his son has led not only to the recovery of his money but also the restoration of his sight and other blessings he could never have imagined before sending his son away.[34] The story shows how Tobit the almsgiver is truly delivered from darkness and death; he is restored to enjoy a full life, thanks to divine intervention in the guise of Tobiah's adventure with an angel. Tobit asks to be "released" and God releases him into life. His story shows the gradual unfolding of God's promise of an abundant life, and Tobit's experience points to the eventual fulfillment of abundant life in the land of milk and honey for Israel.

Earlier in his prayer, Tobit begs the Lord in his poverty. God responds by showing him charity, delivering him from his misfortunes and granting him life. Tobit, in fact, is given a long and prosperous life until a happy old age, with an extended family and seven grandchildren gathered around him as he is dying. His son obeys his instructions and gives him an honorable burial. These are all indicative of a life lived with satisfaction and abundance, of a temporal existence that radiates with fullness and light.

34. Anderson, *Charity*, 81.

Tobit's life proves that charity has such power that it can stir God to restore and raise an individual from death back to life.[35] Tobit has given alms and he receives from God a bountiful life in return.

ALMSGIVING AND THE GOODLY TREASURE

Raphael assures Tobit that it is better to give alms than to store up gold. Why is this so? Tobit's previous assertion that almsgiving allows one to store up a goodly treasure for oneself against the day of adversity can illuminate Raphael's proverbial statement. Prov 19:17, in turn, can elucidate Tobit's reason for almsgiving.

The Book of Proverbs has sayings that recommend openness of heart and hand to the poor (cf. Prov 21:13; 14:21, 31). Prov 19:17, however, is unique in that it states that "he who is generous to the poor lends to the Lord; he will repay him for his charity." The saying views financial gift to the poor as a type of loan made to God; the money given to the poor is conveyed directly to God. Since God is the borrower and the guarantor of the loan, it is secure.[36] Providing a loan is normally a risky undertaking, but when God stands behind a loan, worries of non-payment can be shelved aside. The almsgiver is a creditor who believes in God's creditworthiness. God, in fact, repays the loan in his own time with unimaginable interests that accrue to the principal in the creditor's celestial treasure. Giving alms to the poor can fund one's heavenly treasure. In this view, the outstretched hand of a needy person can be imagined as an "ancient automatic teller machine through which one could make a deposit directly to one's heavenly account."[37] In this way, giving alms to the needy and the downtrodden is a better investment than hoarding gold because it is safer and the divine return is assured, earning the greatest of dividends for the creditor. Hence, almsgiving and charity to the poor benefits not just the recipient of the alms but the donor as well; the needy are aided and enriched while the donor retains both the principal and the interest.[38]

---

35. See Anderson, "Tobit as a Righteous Sufferer," 499–501.

36. Anderson, *Sin*, 165: "The almsgiver becomes a holder of a bond that has been "signed" by God himself. If ordinary investors are partial to the United States treasury notes because the government stands behind them, what about the security one ought to feel if the Holy One of Israel is the borrower?" See also Anderson, *Charity*, 35–52.

37. Anderson, "Redeem Your Sins," 49; Anderson, *Sin*, 142–51.

38. Anderson, *Sin*, 174–76.

In the case of Tobit, his prayer and alms are like loans to God, a record of which is presented to God. His good deeds are securely kept in the heavenly coffers, from which they could be taken out in a time of necessity. His almsgiving has funded his heavenly account to the accrual of interests and dividends. They are later returned to him with the greatest of interests translated as a full and sated life. No wonder that Tobit can claim that such a heavenly treasure will come in handy on the day of need even when, at the time he told his son about it, his situation of darkness seemed to point out the bankruptcy of his celestial funds.

In this understanding, sin is envisaged as debt that can be repaid or wiped out by a withdrawal from the heavenly treasury. No doubt for this reason, Raphael can declare that almsgiving can cleanse sin and can deliver one from death and darkness. In the end, it is indeed better to give alms than to store up gold because alms are secure, with returns guaranteed from God. Unlike storing up gold, alms are a gift that keeps on giving even beyond one's lifetime.

CONCLUDING REMARKS

The Book of Tobit makes pivotal claims regarding almsgiving and works of charity. In his exile, Tobit views almsgiving as enjoying a social and humanitarian value. The horizontal dimension of almsgiving emphasizes the fact that it fosters solidarity among kin and provides mutual aid. More importantly, almsgiving has a theological function because it is a way to remember God. As a vertical act that is referred to God, almsgiving is a worthy offering before the presence of God. The re-consideration of the sacrificial aspect of the cult in terms of almsgiving leads Tobit to claim that almsgiving delivers from darkness and death, that it purges sin, that it is a sure way to fund a heavenly account chargeable on the day of necessity, and that it leads to a divinely favored life. Indeed, Tobit's almsgiving has delivered him from the darkness. God has rewarded Tobit's works of charity with a full life. In sum, the story of Tobit proves that almsgiving possesses redemptive worth.

Of course, such a claim makes better sense if the story of Tobit is read in light of exile. Despite his righteousness and innocence, Tobit's exilic circumstance implicates him in the collective guilt of his people. Tobit's life and that of Israel are intimately intertwined. In fact, Tobit's lament emphasizes his solidarity with his people. Both Tobit and Israel are in the darkness. Given this reality, the story defines the relationship between God and his elect in terms of almsgiving and mercy. Almsgiving and other acts of benevolence are efforts that will expectantly elicit God's response of same, if not greater charity. And so, Tobit's charitable act of gathering and burying the dead will hopefully receive in return God's charitable act of raising Israel from death. In the end, death, burial, almsgiving, and restoration form an intricate interlace that relates to God's outstanding promises to his elect. Before discussing the connections between these theological elements, it is helpful to survey how various scholars have explained the practice of burying the dead, which is deemed an important motif in the narrative discourse of the Book of Tobit.

3

INTERPRETATIONS OF THE SIGNIFICANCE OF BURYING THE DEAD

BURIAL OF THE DEAD is the essential act of almsgiving in the Book of Tobit.[1] That the dead cannot reasonably be expected to repay favors or reward
any good deeds may have constituted the practice of burying the dead as a
paradigmatic act of charity.[2] As Israel Abrahams notes, "charity to the dead
is the type and acme of disinterested love, of disinterested love which, by
the strange ways of Providence, does find its reward."[3]

While it may be true that the story is not chiefly a recommendation
of almsgiving, or its purpose even less so to emphasize the merits of burying the dead,[4] the practice is frequently repeated and so vital an element
in the narrative that "the story would make no sense without the burial
motif."[5] No doubt, Tobit's burial of the dead thrusts the plot of the narrative

---

1. Moore (*Tobit*, 120) claims that it is "the most important act of charity" in the story.
Jensen ("Family," 135) notes that it is "a striking illustration of piety." See also Otzen,
Tobit and Judith, 42; David, "Burial," 492.

2. Olyan ("Israelite Interment Ideology," 609n25) notes that "Israelite (including biblical) evidence for the ability of the dead to act beneficently or malevolently is lacking,
though such data are well attested in surrounding cultures."

3. Abrahams, "Tobit and Genesis," 350.

4. See Schumpp, *Das Buch Tobiah*, xii–xiii.

5. Bolyki, "Burial as an Ethical Task," 99; Nowell, *Narrative Technique*, 201. Ego
("Death and Burial," 87) also acknowledges that burial and death have decisive roles in
the narrative.

forward.[6] Still, the myriad of references to the burial of the dead scattered throughout the narrative demand some other explanation. This chapter analyzes the instances when the story refers to the practice of burying the dead and identifies some common and general features in these episodes. The chapter concludes by surveying how various commentators on the Book of Tobit have made sense of the preponderant presence of this motif in the discourse of the narrative.

EPISODES OF BURYING THE DEAD IN THE BOOK OF TOBIT

The Book of Tobit includes as many as seven episodes that feature interment of dead bodies. In 1:17, Tobit counts burial of his dead kinsmen, whose bodies were thrown over the walls of Nineveh and left for birds of prey to feast on, as an act of charity. Later on, when Sennacherib returned in rage after his setback from Jerusalem and killed many of his exiled kinsmen, Tobit took their bodies by stealth and buried them (1:18). The king was displeased and hunted Tobit down for civil disobedience in order to put him to death. Tobit was able to flee, but his property did not escape confiscation.

In another episode, Tobit asks his son Tobiah to invite the righteous poor among his kin to join him for a meal to celebrate Pentecost (2:1–10). Tobiah returns home with the sad news that one of their people has been murdered. Upon hearing it, Tobit gets up from the dinner table and rushes to bury the dead man despite the insults of his neighbors. Resting in the courtyard afterwards, bird droppings fell directly into his eyes and covered them with white films. Such flawless avian shooting skills render Tobit blind. This episode contributes to the portrait of Tobit's misfortunes and despair, complicating the plot of the story.

In the first case, Tobit defies the decree of the king but observes the divine commandments. The threat to his life and the loss of his property are directly the consequences of this choice. In the second case, it is not clear whether the curious incident of avian marksmanship that blinded him is necessarily connected to his act of burying the dead. And yet, the narrative seems to tie sequentially the event that caused his blindness to his act of burying the remains of a murdered kinsman. Since the first instance of burial in the story has led to Tobit's misfortunes, it is possible that the

---

6. See Efthimiadis-Keith, "The Significance of Food," 557–58.

second instance of Tobit's burial of the dead is also linked to a tragedy, that of his blindness. Another act of kindness ends in another trial.

Tobit's second act of burial and his blindness are not necessarily a convenience of narrative coincidence such as one finds in a Charles Dickens novel; both events are theologically related somehow. These incidents conspire to show that it would be rational for Tobit to cease his acts of compassion to *personae miserae* after the misfortunes and disastrous consequences that seem to accompany them. This poses then the dilemma of whether Tobit will continue in his commitment to bury the dead at this point in the story. That Raphael was sent to test Tobit at that particular time when he did not hesitate to get up and leave his Pentecost dinner to bury the dead, makes better sense in this regard (12:13–14).[7] In actual fact, Tobit persists in the selfless act of burying his dead kin despite multiple personal risks. The lengths that Tobit is willing to go to bury the dead underscore his belief that burial of the dead as an act of charity delivers one from death and leads to a long and fulfilling life (4:10) despite evidence to the contrary. The angel and the story, of course, later confirm the validity of Tobit's commitment and belief.

The remaining five references to burial serve to reinforce its weight in the story. In his wisdom speech to his son, Tobit asks Tobiah to give him an honorable burial after his death, and to honor his mother by burying her next to him (4:3). As a first instruction, Tobit wants nothing more than for his son to practice the self-same act of charity for him and his wife. And so, when Tobiah learns during his journey with Raphael that he is going to marry his kinswoman Sarah, whose seven previous husbands died on their wedding night, Tobiah expresses the concern that if he were to die, no one would give his parents a proper funeral (6:15). More than anything else, Tobiah is worried not about dying but about meeting this filial obligation as his father previously instructed him to do.

When Tobiah and Sarah finally get married, the prospect of another dead husband looms in the air. Fearful of potential insults from the neighbors, Raguel orders his servants to quickly dig a grave for Tobiah (8:18). If Tobiah were to meet the same fate as Sarah's seven previous husbands, the soon-to-be son-in-law could be easily dispatched to the ground in order to prevent anyone from knowing about him, thus avoiding further ridicule and shame. Thankfully, it turns out that both Tobiah and Sarah are alive and fast asleep on their wedding night (8:14).

7. See Anderson, *Charity*, 85–103. But see also Miller, "Raphael the Liar," 492–508.

As the story reaches its dénouement, Raphael reveals to Tobit and To-biah that divine providence has enfolded their lives in a hidden way because Tobit did not hesitate earlier to get up and leave his Pentecost meal behind to bury the dead (12:12–13). Raphael refers to the practice of burying the dead as a test that Tobit surpasses because he has shown his commitment to almsgiving even when it poses risks and leads to distressful results. Through the words of the angel, Tobit's commitment to this particular act of charity earns divine approval.[8] In fact, his prayer and his act of burying the dead turn out to be a memorial that bears Tobit's presence up before God.

At the end of the story, Tobiah honors the wishes of his father. He gives his father an honorable and splendid burial upon his death (14:2). Tobiah also fulfills his obligation to his mother, burying her in one grave next to his father, as Tobit previously commanded him to do. This, of course, follows the ancient Jewish custom of burying the husband and wife together. To-biah does the same for Sarah's parents (14:11b–13). Indeed, Tobiah shows himself to be as adept in the doing of charity and as devoted to the practice of burying the dead as his father Tobit was during his lifetime.

COMMON FEATURES

The episodes of burial in the narrative can be categorized under four head-ings. First, burial of the dead has a theological function in that it is an act of charity that concretizes the remembrance of God and his commands. As an act of compassion, burying the dead is a mark of righteousness and fidelity to the living God.[9] It is certainly an act that violates the law of the king but respects the law of God. Of course, the practice of burial as an act of charity is Tobit's way of reinterpreting and applying the law to new circumstances. That Tobit performs proper burial for the dead in Tobit 1–2 despite risks to his life, isolation, verbal insults, and personal misfortunes shows his loyalty and constant commitment to remember God even in exile. As a practice specifically referred to God, burial becomes a new form of religious piety. His efforts to uphold the law in exile, however, elicit derision even from his fellow Jews (2:7–9).[10] When Raphael reveals the whole truth, Tobit and

---

8. See Macatangay, *Wisdom Instructions*, 108, 170–71.

9. See Macatangay, "Acts of Charity," 69–84.

10. Bolyki ("Burial as an Ethical Task," 97) notes that one of the common features of the practice of burying the dead in Greek tragedies and in the Old Testament is the perception that it shows obedience to the divine law and ancient tradition.

Tobiah learn that this particular expression of charity is a fragrant offering in the sight of God (12:12–15).

Second, Tobit's practice of burying the dead has a sociological import. It is a boundary marker comparable to diet restrictions and endogamy; it helps preserve Jewish identity and the distinctions between Jew and Gentile despite pressure and harassment. If indeed the "prohibition to bury dead Jews is the high point of ancient anti-Judaism,"[11] then burial as a practice reinforces Jewish identity. Tobit as kin bestows the benefit of burial upon the dead as a recognition of their membership into the household of Israel. The practice is a boundary identifier that strengthens the social fabric of Jacob's household.

Third, burial of the dead underscores family ties and kinship. In his discourse to his son, Tobit instructs Tobiah to bury him and his wife in one grave. This charge is similar to Jacob's final command to his sons to bury him where his ancestors are interred (Gen 49:29–32). Tobiah recalls his father's reminder of his filial duty when he expresses his worry to Raphael that his parents would have no family member to perform the funeral rites for them, if he marries Sarah and dies. As the story moves to a close, the narrative seems unnecessarily insistent on the burial of family members. Tobiah buries not only his parents honorably but also the parents of Sarah (14:1,12–13). These instances in the story that refer to the practice of burying the dead provide the impression that burial is, in many ways, tied to family and kin, for the dead are dependent on their kin. Kinship encompasses not only the living members of the household but also the family's departed. The story does not mention any occasion in which a character outside of Tobit's familial network receives burial. Nowhere does Tobit exhort his son to bury someone outside of the family. In fact, Tobit advises his son to offer almsgiving and any act of charity only to the righteous of his own people (4:6; cf. 1:8; 2:2). He specifically instructs Tobiah to be lavish with his bread and wine on the tomb only of the righteous (4:17). That Tobit buries only dead Israelites in the narrative reinforces the significance of kinship that embraces the departed ancestors and the view that burial is an act done for the members of the household. In life as in death, the individual is embedded in the family.

Fourth, burial of the dead is a pointer to life. On the night of the wedding, Raguel summons his servants, ordering them to dig a grave for Tobiah to avoid the ridicule of his prying neighbors. In this episode, the purpose of

---

11. Oeming, "Jewish Identity," 552.

the simple shaft grave dug out of the ground is to hide the body of Tobiah in case of death.[12] Raguel obviously expects Tobiah to meet the fate of death as Sarah's previous seven husbands have. A grave waits to devour the body of Tobiah but the grave proves to be unnecessary in the end. The maid reports that Tobiah is alive and nothing has happened to either Tobiah or Sarah. Raguel thus asks his servants to fill in the grave before dawn (8:18).

This episode occurs at the turning point in the narrative. In fact, if the chiastic structure of the story is laid out, the marriage of Tobiah and Sarah forms the center of the story:[13]

A   Tobit's Words of Instruction (4:1–21)

B   The Journey from Nineveh to Ecbatana (5:1–7:8)

C   The Marriage of Tobiah and Sarah in Ecbatana (7:9—10:13)

B'   The Journey from Ecbatana to Nineveh (11:1—12:22)

A'   Tobit's Words of Praise (13:1—14:2)

The wedding of Tobiah and Sarah, of course, points to the perpetuation of family and life. In the self-same center of the narrative, the covering of the grave functions as a complement since the filling in of the tomb marks the passage from death to life.[14] Because of God's intervention, Tobiah's destiny has changed from death to life.[15] In this case, the empty grave has become instead a sign of life. The marriage and the covered grave are two sides of the same coin—they are parallel intimations of life.

SCHOLARLY INTERPRETATIONS OF THE BURIAL MOTIF

The morbid preoccupation of the narrative with death and burial has elicited various scholarly explanations. The first view may be described as anthropological. The view notes that the story espouses the traditional value

12. See David, "Burial," 493–94.

13. See Engel, "Auf zuverlässigen Wegen," 89–92; Schüngel-Straumann, *Tobit*, 37–38. See also Anderson, "Canonical Ordering of the Twelve," 67, who notes that the travels of the protagonists summarize the plot of Tobit. Certainly, if one looks at the chiastic structure of the book, one notices that travels from Nineveh to Ecbatana and back frame the main event, namely, the wedding of Tobiah and Sarah, which is symbolic of a new beginning and a re-establishment of order and stability after the divine intervention. See also Ravasi, "Il cantico della misericordia," 74–75.

14. Nowell, *Narrative Technique*, 202.

15. See Cousland, "A Comedy in Error," 548–50.

of respect and care for the beloved departed. This demands the practice of burying their bodies. In biblical texts that refer to entombment, burial in the family grave is the most desirable and honorable treatment that the dead can receive while non-burial is the least suitable conduct towards a corpse.[16] Burial is so desired that if a man is childless, he can designate a household member as an "heir" to guarantee himself a proper burial (cf. Gen 15:2). Burial is one of Tobit's major concerns in his discourse to his son (Tob 4:4). Tobiah himself, faced with the possibility of an untimely death if he were to marry Sarah, worries that his parents would have no other son to bury them (Tob 6:15). A corpse that remains unburied is disgraceful and defiling; it is the "worst of all curses."[17] To leave the remains of the deceased subject to the mutilation by birds and animals, denying a dead body the privilege of interment, is to dishonor the deceased.[18] Moreover, to lie unburied after death is a sign of punishment or just desert for one who does not honor God (cf. Jer 8:1–2; Isa 14:19–20; 2 Macc 13:3–8). And so, as Joseph Fitzmyer remarks, Tobit's burial of the dead "reflects the Jewish horror of corpses left unburied, especially those of fellow Jews."[19] To give the deceased a proper funeral is to honor their dignity and to provide them welfare.

The second explanation may be designated as literary. Tobit's practice of interring dead bodies portrays and testifies to his fidelity to ancestral and patriarchal traditions. Indeed, Tobit contravenes the Torah legislation on ritual purity by his contact with corpses. And yet, the recognized norm of respectful burial of family members in the Book of Genesis justifies his faithful adherence to such practice. As Israel Abrahams notes, the Book of Tobit imitates the literary contours and style of Genesis, a book that contains the most number of references to burial of the departed in the biblical corpus.[20] In an attempt to render the character of Tobit with a patriarchal bent, the author introduced burial of the dead, as it is a constant and

16. Olyan, "Israelite Interment Ideology," 603–7.

17. De Vaux, *Ancient Israel*, 56. See, for instance, Deut 28:26; 1 Kgs 14:11; Qoh 6:3; Isa 14:20; Jer 7:33; 16:4; 22:18–19; Ezek 29:5; 39:15; 11QT LXIV 11–12.

18. *Sepulcrum*, from which the word "sepulcher" comes from, is a Latin word that is derived from *sepelire*, which means "to bury." The word also has an Indo-European root that means "to render honor." Burial is etymologically an "honoring gesture" (Harrison, *Dominion of the Dead*, 28).

19. Fitzmyer, *Tobit*, 118.

20. See Gen 23:3–20; 25:9; 35:29; 47:30–31; 49:29–50:14; 50:24–26.

striking feature of patriarchal piety and sensibility.[21] If, on the other hand, it is also true that the Book of Tobit has folktale motifs, the story may echo the tale of the grateful dead. In this story, the hero ransoms at a substantial expense a corpse from a group of creditors who refuse to bury it. The hero provides the body of the deceased its burial for which he is later rewarded. Such literary strands, both biblical and non-biblical, may explain the strong presence of the burial motif in the story. Still, this does not fully explain the purpose or the function of the inclusion of the burial motif in the narrative.

The third view may be described as historical. This view suggests that the importance of burying the dead in Tobit arose from certain historical circumstances and influences. The plays of Sophocles such as *Antigone* and *Ajax* suggest that burial of the dead is a significant aspect of the Greek ethic.[22] The duty to bury the dead is clearly not entirely Greek, though the particular attention in the story given to the duty of burial may nonetheless reflect Hellenistic influences.[23] On the other hand, if Tobit is deemed a novel of apologetics whose Greek translation came from Egypt, it might be possible to treat the theme of burial as a polemic against the Egyptian practice of mummification.[24]

The fourth explanation may be labeled ethical. In this view, the burial of the dead in the Book of Tobit addresses the moral calculus of reward and punishment. According to János Bolyki, burial of the dead is an ethical task that moves in three directions: "obedience towards God, piety towards outsiders and setting an example and assuming solidarity, strengthening the internal cohesion towards the members of the people."[25] Tobit remains faithful to this ethical norm despite the personal pain that it entails in practice. The story thus shows that such fidelity to the law is never in vain, even when this is not instantly clear. Eventually it would earn the obedient practitioner divine favors, as Tobit's case shows. Beate Ego seems to agree with Bolyki's assessment, seeing in this practice the crises as well as the validity of the deed-consequence theology. For her, "one of the most important messages of the story" is "the validity of an intramundane justice in which

21. Abrahams, "Tobit and Genesis," 349–50. See also Fitzmyer, *Tobit*, 118. Efthimiadis-Keith ("The Significance of Food," 553–78) notes that along with food and eating, the burial of the dead contributes to the development of Tobit's character.

22. See Garland, *The Greek Way of Death*, 21–37, 104–20.

23. See Crouch, *Origin and Intention*, 74n9.

24. See Schwartz, "Remarques littéraire," 297.

25. Bolyki, "Burial as an Ethical Task," 100.

act and consequence bear a reciprocal relation to each other."[26] Abrahams in that short essay of long ago also included this estimation in his evaluation of this practice in Tobit. The story endorses the lesson that burial of the dead is "the very charity of truth" which is to be followed whatever the results are. For in addition to virtue being its own recompense, it will also be profitably rewarded.[27]

CONCLUDING REMARKS

The various interpretations of why burial of the dead is important in the Book of Tobit may be grouped into four categories: anthropological, literary, historical, and ethical. From the survey of the many instances in which burial of the deceased is either portrayed or referred to in the story, it has become evident that the narrative primarily views Tobit's activity of burying the dead as a concrete act of charity that shows his mindfulness of God while he is in exile. Tobit's practice, which is also a marker of identity, proves his obedience to God's commands rather than to the laws of the king. The story also links the practice of burying the departed with kin and the household. Finally, the digging of the grave on the wedding night of Tobiah and Sarah gives the impression that burial of the dead hints at life.

26. Ego, "Death and Burial," 101.
27. Abrahams, "Tobit and Genesis," 350.

4

BURIAL OF THE DEAD, KIN, AND LAND

SENNACHERIB KILLED THE ISRAELITES in revenge for his defeat and they lie scattered on the streets of Nineveh. Seven husbands are dead on their wedding night before the marriage can be consummated. Tobit and Sarah pray for death. And Tobiah is dismissed as lost, dead with a grave lying in wait for him. Such palpable presence of death in the story makes the insistent narrative pulse on the activity of burying the dead hardly surprising. With so many dead bodies, interment becomes a necessary activity. After all, death and burial are closely connected; they form part of a continuum with burial concluding the process of death on this side of the grave. Life is brought to completion not in death but in burial. It is for this reason that burial of the dead is essential in the biblical worldview.

At the same time, the narrative struggles with the crisis of exile. The first and the last two chapters (Tobit 1–2; 13–14) that structurally frame the narrative deal with exile. The story introduces Tobit as he struggles to live a life in captivity and it closes with the note that his descendants are still on the move, living away from the land. The interlocking individual stories of Tobit, Sarah, and Tobiah in the middle of the narrative find not only continuity but also allusive resonances in the opening and closing chapters of the story. Their personal fates are a dramatic illustration of "the incongruities of the dystopic world" to "its systemic restoration," which takes place by means of three basic narrative inversions: (1) the relation of men and women, (2) the relation of humans to animals, and (3) the relation of humans to God's retributive justice, with the "subjection of a scattered

Israel to the rule of powerful Gentiles" as the central inversion.[1] The exilic circumstance of Israel reveals the striking inconsistency between the divine purpose and the historical reality in the same way that death is inharmonious with the life-giving intention of the God of life. Death, as refracted in the individual tragedies of the main characters, encompasses exile. In fact, exile and death stand in close parallel, implying that rescue from one is also rescue from the other.

The narrative proffers the perception that the exilic condition has driven Tobit to perform burial for his dead compatriots. Tobit rescues the corpses of murdered Jews left exposed under the sun and consequently contravenes the Mosaic prohibition against contaminating contact with dead bodies (Lev 21:1–4; 22:4; Num 19:11–16; Hag 2:13). Why would Tobit risk ritual impurity by singlehandedly burying the dead? The fact of exile may be a critical factor to consider in responding to such a question. Burial practice and ideology that typified the Israelite experience may also elucidate the hidden or assumed aspects of burial in the story. This chapter attempts to look at the practice of burying the dead and its attendant ideology as it pertains to the problem of exile.

SLEEPING WITH THE ANCESTORS

The description for the physical act of burial or interment in family tombs often employs such idiomatic expressions as "to be gathered to/come to/lie down/sleep with one's ancestors/people" (cf. Gen 15:15, 25:8; 2 Kgs 20:21).[2] These vivid idioms suggest the idea that the dead individual is brought to some kind of proximity with the deceased kin at burial. To be buried is to be reconnected with those who have gone before; it is literally to be in the company of the ancestors. These expressions for burial hint at the close familial and kinship relations that survive death despite the changed existence. In short, burial of the dead is a practice driven by the primacy of family and kinship in life and in death.

Where does Tobit bury the dead? Where does he take the victims of the king to sleep with their ancestors? The story does not mention a specific

1. Cousland, "Comedy in Error," 548–51.

2. See Hallotte, *Death, Burial and the Afterlife*, 43. De Vaux, *Ancient Israel*, 59, notes that the idiom originally referred to the "custom of a family tomb, but the original meaning later took on a deeper sense, and the words became a solemn formula signifying death, and at the same time emphasizing that the ties of blood reached beyond the grave."

place or family graves as locations of burial. The reader does not know if Tobit buries the dead in a family tomb or in a substitute place located away from the property holding of the family. The story, however, emphasizes the fact that Tobit treats his dead co-religionists respectfully with burial. In fact, by burying the dead, Tobit treats them as if they were family members. Despite the absence of reference to any family tomb, Tobit's burial of the dead underscores the importance of kinship ties and family relations and the link that continues to exist beyond the grave between the living and the dead. That Tobit asks his son to bury him and his wife (4:4) in one grave implies that the dimensions of family relationships continue to abide in the afterlife.

In the fictional universe of the story, every character is related as a brother or sister. Tobit calls his wife Hannah "sister" (5:21) as Raguel does his wife Edna (7:15) and Tobiah his wife Sarah (8:4, 7). Azariah calls Tobit "brother" (5:11) and Tobit addresses him as "brother" in response (5:14). Raphael calls Tobiah "brother" (6:11, 12) and Tobiah responds in kind (6:7, 14; 7:9; 9:2). Edna calls her future son-in-law Tobiah "brother" (10:13). In exile, all Israelites belong to one household. In this way, the story adheres to the biblical belief that the individual self is "socially embedded" and inextricably entwined with kin and family.[3] Tobit's burial of his fellow deceased Israelites reinforces the view of Israel as one extended family. As the male kin, Tobit has become the household's undertaker *par excellence*, taking on the primary responsibility of burying the dead of Israel in exile. His practice reflects fictively the familial relations and preserves the corporate identity of Israel. It shows his "loyalty to an entire people conceived of as family"—"Jews treating other Jews as family."[4]

Moreover, the ties of the dispersed dead to the household of Jacob continue to hold after death in and beyond the grave. In other words, Tobit's activity of burial views the household of Israel as a collective in which the relationship of the deceased to the living members of the household is perpetuated. In Tobit's world, burial makes it possible to reflect that what is true above the ground in terms of Israel's kinship and communal identity also applies below the ground.

Tobit's performance of burial for those slain by Sennacherib functions as a figurative integration of the victims of the king into the people of

---

3. See De Vito, "Construction of Personal Identity, 221–25. See also Levenson, *Resurrection and the Restoration of Israel*, 109.

4. Soll, "Window on the Hellenistic Jewish Family," 274.

Israel.[5] In Tobit's hands, those who die outside the land, die like Abraham, buried, or as the biblical idiom goes, "gathered to his people" and "reunited with one's own." Burial is the assertion that their death in a foreign land neither results in the loss of their identity nor severs their relationship with their kin nor ends their belonging to Israel's household. In this regard, the burial of the dead is a practice that captures and reflects the solidarity of Israel as a family even in exile. To provide burial is to claim that all the scattered righteous dead understood as kin are gathered and symbolically restored into the house of Jacob.

In its use of images, Tobit's prophetic prediction for the ingathering of Israel echoes the importance of kinship. In his final testament, Tobit calls Jerusalem the house of God for all ages (14:5). The rebuilding of the city of Jerusalem as God's eternal house is metaphorically tied to the restoration of Israel as the household of God. In short, it is as a household that Israel is rebuilt. In his praise, Tobit calls himself blessed if a "remnant of his offspring" or a member of his family is left to see the glory of God's house (13:16). Tobit is aware that his prophetic words will be fulfilled after his death. Since burial incorporates the dispersed dead into the house of Jacob from which Tobit's remnant will arise, Tobit's hopes of rebuilding are not in vain. For the descendants of Tobit to experience the glory of God's restored house is for Tobit himself to experience the fulfillment of God's promise. When the restoration of the household of Israel takes place in the land of the ancestors, the buried dead of Israel would have equally enjoyed the realization of the divine promise in their descendants.

If this is correct, it is no wonder that the story understands Tobit's practice of burying the dead in exile as an act of rebellion deserving of capital punishment (1:18–20). Burial is an act of kinship that gathers what is scattered and lost. The activity of burial is Tobit's emblematic gesture of counteracting the dissolution and decomposition of the house of Israel. Burial can thus be viewed as a political act that protests and thwarts the king's intent to kill many Israelites out of rage or revenge (cf. Tob 1:18).

Finally, Tobit's burial of the dead rectifies the shameful public display of Jewish corpses. To allow the exposure of the remains of the Jewish victims signifies far more than disregard for them. It may also denote the extension of punishment beyond death into the afterlife.[6] To provide them burial is to give them rest from punishment after death. If exile is viewed

5. See Ego, "Death and Burial," 90, 99.
6. See Brichto, "Kin, Cult, Land and Afterlife," 36.

as a chastisement (cf. 3:4; 13:5; 14:4–7), then Tobit's activity of burying the dead may be taken as a hint or a foreshadowing of the end of the punishment for dead Israel. In Tobit's burial activities, God's people can discern that rest in the land is close at hand.

JOSEPH'S BONES AND TOBIT

The Book of Genesis is often credited with informing the theological and literary imagination behind the narrative world of Tobit. It has been said that the Joseph cycle of stories (Gen 37–50) in particular share similarities with Tobit.[7] Only a couple of the parallels are necessary for our purposes— both the stories of Joseph and Tobit are set outside the land and both stress the significant role of burial. Joseph asks pharaoh to allow him to bury his father Jacob in the grave prepared for him in the land of Canaan, obeying thus the deathbed charge of his father (Gen 49:30–32; 50:1–14). In a similar fashion, Tobiah gives his father Tobit a proper and honorable funeral after his death, showing that he has indeed heeded the specific instruction his father previously gave him. As Joseph was dying, he assured his brothers that God will take care of them and commanded them to bring his bones from Egypt (cf. Gen 50:24–26). Before his breath failed him, Tobit also promised Tobiah and his children that God would have mercy on them and bring them back to the land of Israel (Tob 14:5) after which, the story notes that Tobit received an honorable burial. At the very least, these elements show the critical importance of proper burial for the dead. In the case of Joseph and Jacob, proper burial means burial in the family tomb. Might this also be the case with Tobit's instruction to Tobiah to provide him a proper burial?

Joseph's command to carry his bones is tied to God's remembrance of his people. The verb פקד in Gen 50:24–26, which is often translated as "to take care/take notice," can also have the sense of "to remember" as in the case of Gen 21:1 in which God "takes notice" or "remembers" Sarah.[8] Like Joseph, Tobit does not doubt that God would remember his people and his covenant promises, claiming that those who reside outside the land who remember and sincerely put into practice the divine words could hope to be gathered in the land in the fullness of time (Tob 13:13; 14:5–7). When God remembers and visits his people to give them the land promised to

7. See Ruppert, "Das Buch Tobias," 113–17. See also the comments of Anderson, *Charity*, 78–82.

8. André, "פקד *pāqad*," 54–55.

the patriarchs, Joseph expects that his descendants would remember him by bringing his mortal remains for safekeeping to the family grave in the homeland. This human action of carrying the bones of Joseph from Egypt to the land, however, can be viewed, as Sir 49:15 does, as a "divinely activated proof that God had been true to his promises."[9]

In a prayer that begs for death (3:6), recited just before instructing Tobiah to give him a proper burial (4:1–2), Tobit asks God to remember him. Such request for remembrance may include the hope of being brought and laid to rest in the family tomb, to be gathered with kin in the land after his death. Moreover, Tobit and Hannah refer to their son Tobiah as "the light of my eyes," a metaphorical expression that evokes not only life and vitality but also a whole series of descendants (cf. Prov 20:20; 24:20) who will continue Tobit's line that, in turn, will ensure their proper care after their deaths.[10] Would these hints point to the possibility that Tobit, like Joseph, expects his final rest to be in the family grave in the land when God remembers and visits his people?

The saga of Joseph's bones continues in the Book of Exodus, many themes of which find echoes in the Book of Tobit.[11] Exodus notes that Moses, despite a departure from Egypt that is so hasty as to leave the bread unleavened, was able to take Joseph's remains with him, remembering the charge Joseph had given to the Israelites to bury his bones in a family gravesite (Exod 13:19). This detail makes it appear that the Exodus out of Egypt is a long funeral procession in search of a burial ground, that indeed the land of promise has a mortuary landscape. Joseph would eventually find his final resting place in Shechem in the land of Canaan (cf. Josh 24:32) in a plot of land Jacob previously bought and where he invoked the name of the God of Israel (cf. Gen 33:18–20).

The significance of this passing note in Exodus lies in disclosing a key stage in the drama of God's promises to the Israelites and in the journey that reaches its conclusion in the burial of Joseph's bones in the land (Josh 24:32). The descent of Israel into Egypt, the house of bondage, begins with a conflict among the sons of Jacob. As a result of his brothers' hatred and jealousy, Joseph ends up in Egypt. Through Joseph, God secures the lives and the survival of the remnant of Israel on earth (cf. Gen 45:5–8; 50:20).

9. Hayward, "*Multum in Parvo*," 190.

10. On the idea of light as equivalent to line of heirs, see Brichto, "Kin, Cult, Land and Afterlife," 33–34.

11. See Macatangay, "Election by Allusion," 450–63.

And so, to bring Joseph's bones out of Egypt provides continuity and closure to the story and fate of the Israelites in the house of slavery. It symbolizes the fact that what God began with Joseph has now been marvelously accomplished: God's mysterious providential involvement in the affairs of the brothers has kept Israel alive.

The place of burial in the story of Joseph is significant. In Gen 46:3–4, God speaks to Jacob, Joseph's father, and assures him that it is safe to go to Egypt. God himself promises to go down with Jacob to Egypt and to bring him back to his land. Jacob, of course, dies in Egypt but his body is promptly brought back to Canaan for burial under Joseph's direction. This human action is evidence enough that God's promise to Jacob to bring him back to his land is fulfilled immediately after his death. This is not the case with Joseph, however, at least not at this stage. As Genesis concludes with the death of Joseph, his embalmed body remains in Egypt. One would naturally expect that Joseph's body would also be brought immediately back to Canaan right after his death, as is the case with Jacob his father. Instead, Joseph obtains a promise from the sons of Israel to bring his bones with them when God remembers and visits them in order to take them to the land of their fathers, thus binding them and future generations to an action that is contingent upon God's action. That Joseph's bones are finally buried in the land after almost four hundred years is a sign of God's remembrance of his people and fulfillment of his promises to the Israelites. In the descendants of Joseph, God fulfilled his word.

In his instructions, Tobit nowhere asks for his bones to be carried home from exile, although he does ask for a proper burial. With lively hopes of return to the land based on his own experience of divine assistance, Tobit is sure that God will take care of his people. With Joseph's statement to his brothers in mind, Tobit's hopes would seem to imply a similarly strong desire to have his bones interred in the family tomb, which is likely located in his homeland. The narrative does not say whether Tobit has purchased a parcel of real estate as a family tomb in his land of exile. Since Tobit is an orphan in exile from the north, one can perhaps assume that the family tomb where his parents are interred is in the land (cf. 1:8). If indeed a connection between proper burial and the condition of happiness of the deceased exists in the afterlife,[12] then Tobit's burial in the family grave would ensure and prolong his felicity in the hereafter.

---

12. See Brichto, "Kin, Cult, Land and Afterlife," 8.

The story does note that Tobit is buried in Nineveh (14:2). Tobiah buries his in-laws in Ecbatana in Media (14:13). As Tobit looks forward to God's visitation and restoration of Israel, Tobit asks his son Tobiah to flee and to take his grandchildren to Media before Nineveh is destroyed (14:3). After this prophetic word against Nineveh,[13] the narrative concludes with the family of Tobit still on the move, instilled with hopes that in the appointed time of God's restoration, the family will make the final move into the land of promise when what God has said through his prophets will be fulfilled, since "not a single word of the prophecies will fail" (14:4). In the meantime, Tobit's experience of God's care provides the assurance that the prophetic predictions will come true; his family's permanent claim on the land will take place in the plenitude of time. In light of such expressed hopes, a sense of the temporary hovers over and surrounds the burials of the characters as the story ends.

Informed by the traditions of burial in Genesis and Exodus, the burial of Tobit and all the scattered dead outside of the land, like Joseph's burial in Egypt, signals the temporary loss of claim on God's promises. But divine providence, which was operative in the time of Joseph, is at work still in the days of Tobit. Just as the hand of divine providence guided Joseph's descent into Egypt, so too it accompanied Tobit's descent into the darkness of exile. As is evident in the drama of God's veiled and providential aid to Tobit and his family while experiencing misfortunes in foreign lands, God remembers and continues to abide with his people, albeit mysteriously. When God remembers his people, rescuing Israel from captivity and restoring the family of Jacob to the Promised Land, Tobit seems to expect to have his mortal remains gathered and transferred for burial in the land. If Tobit's descendants do so, in the same way that Moses and Joseph's descendants collected and carried the bones of Joseph from Egypt to provide them a resting place in the family land, it would show that not one single righteous Israelite is left behind when God comes to free his people from the world of darkness.

Joseph's descendants assiduously carried out his dying wish. They remarkably adhered to an ancient oath through thick and thin for hundreds of years. Early interpreters explain the textual insistence for why the Israelites kept their vow and punctiliously executed Joseph's charge in terms

---

13. In the longer Greek recension, the prophecy is attributed to Nahum. In the shorter Greek recension, the prophecy is Jonah's. See Estes, "Place of the Gentiles," 65–66.

of his exceptional virtue, wisdom, and conduct.[14] The logic seems to be that if Joseph were not virtuous in every way, the Israelites would not have bothered to take his bones with them. In fact, among the various narrative elements associated with Joseph, Ben Sira picks up this particular detail on the care of Joseph's bones in his praise of the fathers (cf. Sir 49:15), a notable fact that the Second Temple cosmopolitan sage from Jerusalem must have viewed as a testimony to Joseph's exceptional virtue. The story of Tobit, of course, equally portrays the main character as an exemplar of righteousness and wisdom, a virtuous individual unsullied by the heretical actions of his tribe. Tobit has also limited acts of charity to the righteous poor, implying that the dead recipients of burial in the story possess righteous character. In this light, burial in the land may be viewed as related to the excellence of virtue and righteousness. Biblically, all those who served God loyally are provided burial.[15] Similarly, Tobit and all the righteous Israelites who die outside the land can expect their descendants, as Joseph did, to provide them burial in their family graves when God takes notice and comes to them. As kin, Tobit's descendants share in the promise and the responsibility to bring and bury the bones of the dead in the family grave to signify that they indeed have gone to their ancestors in peace. After all, kinship implicates the members of the family in the fate of the others. In this way, the divine promise of land to those who walk with God is fulfilled even after death.

To summarize, Jacob longed and expressly requested to be buried in the family grave (cf. Gen 49:29; 50:5). God promised him that God himself would take him to the land after Joseph had closed his eyes (Gen 46:4). Joseph, his son, extricated an oath from his brothers to bury him in the family grave. To be buried in the family tomb is to return to the land and to be gathered with the ancestors. The burial of the patriarchs shares the commonality of being buried in the family grave (cf. Gen 25:9–10). If the Book of Genesis has indeed influenced the Book of Tobit, it is likely that Tobit's desire for a proper burial also implies a desire to be re-interred in the family grave. The land of Israel could be understood as the family grave writ large. Such a desire conforms to the biblical tradition that views burial outside the land as a curse (cf. Jer 20:6).

---

14. Kugel, *In Potiphar's House*, 125–29. See also Hayward, "*Multum in Parvo*," 185–200; Corley, "Joseph as Exemplar," 157–78.

15. See Bloch-Smith, *Judahite Burial Practices*, 112.

SECONDARY BURIAL IN FAMILY GRAVES

The idiomatic expressions "to be gathered to his kinsfolk" and "to lay with the fathers" have been suggested to refer as well to the Second Temple period practice of secondary burial, which is the collection, transfer, and reburial of mortal remains after the decomposition of the flesh in a new place of repose; the dead are gathered to their ancestors as their remains literally lie on a pile of ancestral bones in the burial chamber of the family or communal grave.[16] Archaeological findings have unearthed many ossuaries and repositories that contain remains of wealthy Jews from the Diaspora buried in and around Jerusalem.[17] Admittedly, the rise of the use of individual ossuaries, receptacles, and bone containers dates to the late first century BCE and early first century CE. Still, collective secondary burials in pits, underground chambers, niches, and caves are said to be typical in the region.[18] Sizable family tombs would employ a chamber as a charnel room for the secondary disposal of the dead. Although secondary burial had undergone some variations over time, local traditions in Palestine regarded it as normal practice.[19] Despite the change in practice over time, the ideological significance of secondary and collective burials remained in place.

The Book of Tobit nowhere mentions secondary burial practices. However, it is not unlikely that the custom of secondary burial taken as the practice of rejoining the ancestors in the family or communal tomb in death informs the imagination of the story. If this burial practice were indeed normal custom so much so that the narrative assumes the reader's knowledge of it, then it would be unnecessary for the story to describe burial practices in a detailed or explicit way. The desire for a proper burial would involve such a practice and assume such an ideology. If this is true, Tobit performs primary burial for the deceased at the time of their death

16. See Meyers, *Jewish Ossuaries*, 14: "The biblical phrase "to be gathered to one's fathers" undoubtedly betrays the realia of secondary burial customs—the dead were in a very real sense gathered to their families in the grave." See Meyers, "Secondary Burials in Palestine," 15. See also Bloch-Smith, *Judahite Burial Practices*, 37.

17. See Meyers, *Jewish Ossuaries*, 11, 37–39, 72–74.

18. See McCane, *Roll Back the Stone*, 42–47.

19. McCane ("Death and Burial," 265) notes that the Book of Tobit "serves as a reminder that the realities of daily life and death in Hellenistic Palestine did not always allow for traditional practices of burial in underground chambers. When circumstances did permit it, however, it was expected that primary burial in an underground chamber would later be followed by secondary burial." See also Hachlili, *Jewish Funerary Customs*, 483–84.

in temporary tombs in or near the location of their death. When the flesh of the dead has wasted away, their skeletal remains are collectively gathered and transferred to the family tomb for their final rest and where the dead may be provided post-mortem provisions.[20] In fact, Tobit's instruction that recommends lavish deeds for the righteous dead (4:17) would make sense against this backdrop of secondary burials in underground chambers.[21]

Burial in the family tomb is said to preserve "the succession of the generations in a traditional society."[22] Burial grounds can therefore serve as road maps for genealogical tracing. In this regard, the genealogy that opens the Book of Tobit serves a purpose parallel to that of interment in the family tomb. On one hand, Tobit's genealogy identifies the lineage of his clan (1:1–2). On the other hand, a communal tomb contains the amassed remains of the generations of his family. Genealogy and the use of family tomb by a kinship group convey the same function in that both reify collective identity. They both point to the "house of the father." In other words, this practice of burial and its attendant ideology accord well with the narrative claims regarding kinship among the dispersed of Israel.

Even if only by allusion or indirect reference, the activity of burying the dead in the narrative may be assuming the ideology that pertains to the practice of secondary burial. There is a likely intimation of this possibility and desire for secondary burial in the family tomb in Tobit's instruction that he and his wife be buried in one grave, which is presumably a family tomb (4:4; 14:2). Tobit's command betrays the same patriarchal need to be buried with family members (cf. Gen 23:19–20). Such preference is equally reflected in Isaiah's reprimand of Shebna who chose a grandiose individual tomb in Jerusalem instead of burial with his family members (Isa 22:16). In view of exile and Tobit's belief that his fellow dispersed co-religionists are all kin, burial with family members may mean reburial in the land. For Tobit then, burial in the land may be described as interment in the family sepulcher writ large; the land is the family burial chamber where the dispersed dead rejoin the ancestors. No doubt, for one who has devotedly

---

20. See Bloch-Smith, "Cult of the Dead," 213–22; Bloch-Smith, *Judahite Burial Practices*, 105; Johnston, *Shades of Sheol*, 62–64.

21. Two meals are interrupted in the story. The first is Tobit's Pentecost meal, which he left in order to bury the dead. The second is the wedding feast that was interrupted to prepare a grave for Tobiah. According to MacDonald, these episodes show a "conjunction of food being abandoned ('poured out') for the sake of the dead" ("Bread on the Grave," 103).

22. Hachlili, *Jewish Funerary Customs*, 310.

made pilgrimages to Jerusalem and expects the city to be rebuilt, for one who displays such depth of commitment to Jerusalem, for someone who is from the land,[23] a desire to rest in the land with kin would be enough of a motivation for the reburial of his mortal remains in the family grave understood as the land. Like Jacob and Joseph, Tobit is an Israelite born in the land who wishes to have his remains returned to the land and buried with his ancestors.[24] To a certain extent, Tobit's reburial would rectify his exilic displacement; through reburial, he would have died like his ancestors gathered to their kin in the land.

When episodes of burial in the narrative are examined closely, telling details are notably absent. The narrative seems to presume that the reader would have some familiarity with aspects that are related to the burial of the dead. Tobit, for instance, mentions simply that whenever one of his people had died and was thrown outside the walls of Nineveh, he would bury them (1:17). Questions arise: how exactly does Tobit do that? And where does he bury them? Doubtless, Tobit does not bury them in pagan cemeteries. After Tobiah informs him that one of his kinsmen has been murdered with the body lying in the marketplace, Tobit rushes to bury the deceased before sunset (2:4, 7). The time detail gives the impression that the custom presumed in the story is that burial has to take place promptly on the same day or as soon as possible after death because exposed dead bodies are unsettling to Jewish sensibilities (cf. Deut 21:23; Josh 10:26–27). This episode seems to assume as well that it takes a short period of time for Tobit, despite being alone, to bury the deceased. Similar observations can be made with regard to another instance of burial in the story. On the wedding night of Tobiah and Sarah, Raguel commands his servants to dig a grave in the event that they have to hide the body of Tobiah after his death so as to avoid the neighbor's curiosity and further ridicule.[25] Tobiah, of course, survives the fateful evening. Finding out that Tobiah is alive, Raguel instructs his

23. Gafni ("Reinterment in the Land of Israel," 97–98) notes that in later instances of transferring remains for burial in the land such as Aristobolus II, the son of Alexander Jannaeus, Matitya son of Judah, R. Meir, Queen Helena and her son Izates, the dead was either a resident of the land or had prior contact with the land and for some other reason, died abroad.

24. See Gafni, *Land, Center, Diaspora*, 84, noting that the biblical examples of Jacob and Joseph are a precedent that "fits practically all the examples of a similar practice in Second Temple times."

25. In the short Greek recension of 8:9, Raguel himself went out alone to dig the grave for Tobiah.

servants to fill in the grave before dawn to keep up appearances (8:18). Here, as in the burial that Tobit earlier afforded a murdered Israelite before becoming blind, the dead are dispatched to the grave in the easiest and quickest way possible. The time duration of the burial depicted in these scenes is rather short, "only maybe a few hours to prepare a grave, which in this case, could only be a simple shaft grave dug out of the ground."[26]

Would this be the kind of honorable burial that Tobit asks his son to perform for him (4:4)? If proper burial is so important for Tobit, it is likely that something more than inhumation in a simple shaft grave in the ground is imagined. If burial in shaft graves would indeed preclude "sleeping" or "being gathered with the ancestors,"[27] then another form of burial might be in view. Moreover, if the commandment to honor one's parents (cf. Exod 20:12) truly includes the respect to be shown to parents not only in life but also after their death,[28] then Tobiah has the filial obligation to provide his parents burial in the family grave.[29] In fact, Tobit echoes the command in Deut 5:16 to honor father and mother when he instructs Tobiah to honor his mother and to bury her with him. Remarkably, Deuteronomy relates the commandment with long life in the land. Tobit seems to understand the divine command to honor one's parents to include the obligation of properly burying him and his wife (Tob 4:4). For Tobiah to bury his parents in shaft graves can imply a consequent lack of care and respect on his part; it can mean that Tobiah has not observed his father's command to bury him and his wife in one grave. To impart this kind of respect and honor for parents after their death would assume that Tobiah has upheld his filial duty of maintaining ownership of the family tomb. As Tobit's son and descendant in exile, Tobiah accomplishes this duty when he returns to claim the land understood as the place for gathering the ancestors of Israel's household to their kin.

26. Dávid, "Burial," 494.

27. Bloch-Smith, *Judahite Burial Practices*, 111.

28. See Brichto, "Kin, Cult, Land and Afterlife," 20–32. See also de Vaux, *Ancient Israel*, 61; and Bloch-Smith, *Judahite Burial Practices*, 112. Levenson, *Resurrection and the Restoration of Israel*, notes that there is "lack of evidence" to support this claim.

29. Hachlili, *Jewish Funerary Customs*, 310, notes of family burial: "The children, the younger generation, were eager to continue the tradition, especially to fulfill their proper and ceremonial duties, adding memorial inscriptions to the interred, designating their status, their family relationship, and sometimes their occupation, title, and so on. They were obliged to protect their ancestors and family status, by guarding the site of the tomb and the position of those buried in the grave. The family tomb was considered a house and the necropolis as the city of the dead."

Now, if Robert Littmann is correct that "proper burial" means "with due rites,"[30] the instruction of Tobit to his son to bury him well becomes intelligible against the background of secondary burials. It appears likely then that Tobit's desire for an honorable burial includes the intention or desire to perform the sacred act and duty of transferring his remains into the family tomb in the land of his ancestors for final interment when circumstances allow it, that is, when God remembers and visits his people. Since the "most honorable burials are those conducted in family ancestral tombs," Tobit's request for a proper burial may point to reburial in the land understood as the ancestral grave.[31]

What rites are performed at secondary burials? Rabbinic literature may be able to shed some light on rituals specific to proper burial. Rabbinic texts such as the tannaitic tractate *Semahot* and the Mishnah *Mo'ed Qatan* are admittedly late, but these are typically considered to contain fairly accurate descriptions of early Jewish burial practices. In these texts, secondary burial, which takes place about one year after death and burial, is the final act in the Jewish ritual of mourning for the dead before normal life resumes. In *Semahot* 12:9, the son has the obligation to collect and provide a second burial to the bones of his father:

> Rabbi Eleazar bar Zadok said: "Thus spoke father at the time of his death: 'My son, bury me first in a fosse. In the course of time, collect my bones and put them in an ossuary; but do not gather them with your own hands.' And thus I did attend to him: Johanan entered, collected the bones, and spread a sheet over them. I then came in, rent my clothes for them, and sprinkled dried herbs over them. Just as he attended his father, so I attended him."

If the custom of secondary burial indeed lies behind Tobit's instruction to his son to bury him well, Tobiah has the responsibility of making sure that Tobit's reburial takes place as the last act in a prescribed rite of mourning. After the bones are collected and reburied, the mourning rituals are concluded. Once the transfer of bones has transpired, it is forbidden to remove them again. If these burial and mourning rituals are performed for Tobit, then Tobit would have indeed received a proper and honorable funeral, a burial with due rites, as he has wished. It is likely then that there is a

30. Littmann, *Tobit*, 87.

31. Stern, "Death and Burial," 272: "Only covenant violators and enemies (1 Kgs 14:11; Jer 14:16; Deut 28:6) are punished with disinterment, dishonorable burial, or lack of burial."

narrative expectation that Tobit's descendants will carry out his secondary burial in the land understood as the family and ancestral grave.

FAMILY GRAVES AND LAND POSSESSION

Burial in the family grave is critical to land possession and perpetuation. Inhumation in the family grave speaks to an ideology in which ancestral tombs bolster the family claim to the inheritance, constituting a "physical, perpetual witness to ownership of the land."[32] The family sepulcher provides legitimacy to patrimonial claims. In Genesis 23, for instance, the story of Abraham's negotiation with the Hittites to purchase a parcel of land at Machpelah to bury Sarah emphasizes the territorial function of burial grounds. In her analysis of this biblical episode, Francesca Stavrakopoulou notes that two concepts of territorial acquisition are in play, namely the notion that the land as commodity can be bought and the idea that the land is an ancestral holding.[33] While Abraham's purchase of the land betrays his status as a resident immigrant, the burial of Sarah's body in a tomb in the purchased land marks the place as an ancestral home. Interment of the dead in a grave suggests territoriality, transforming the land into an exclusive, inalienable, and permanent possession protected from future sale. In short, the grave of the dead marks the family land on behalf of the living descendants. To bury the dead in a particular place is "the surest way to take possession of a place and secure it as one's own."[34] As such, Abraham's purchase of a piece of land to bury the remains of Sarah and Jacob's purchase of a land in Gen 33:19, where Joseph's bones ultimately are buried, presage the possession of the land of Canaan by Abraham's later descendants.

Tobit's desire to be buried in the land is a strong re-assertion of the claim on the divine promise of land possession. It is to keep faith regarding the inheritance of the land. The insistence on burial in the narrative suggests the idea of land as a permanent family property with an ancestral tomb that functions as "a physical marker of the family claim to the land."[35] Tobit's burial of the dead and the reasonable hopes of giving the dispersed

---

32. Bloch-Smith, "Cult of the Dead," 222.

33. Stavrakopoulou, *Land of our Fathers*, 33–38.

34. Harrison, *Dominion of the Dead*, 24.

35. Bloch-Smith, *Judahite Burial Practices*, 111. She also notes that "beginning with the conquest generation, burials were located in the family inheritance."

dead of Israel a final resting place in the land of promise creates the sense that the land will be landscaped with the dead of Israel, marking that acre of earth an inalienable possession and perpetual inheritance of Israel.

Why would the story express such a desire? First, the narrative seems to argue that in addition to the observance of the Torah of Moses, as it is filtered through the instructions of Tobit, the other element of identity and belonging for Diaspora Jews who die outside the land is burial in the land understood as the ancestral grave. Second, the eschatology espoused in the story embraces not only a temporal but also a spatial dimension.[36] As Tobit proclaims in the prophetic element of his farewell discourse, God will show Israel his mercy and will bring those scattered among the Gentiles back to the land of Israel (13:3–6), rebuilding his house as his home forever when the time of fulfillment comes (cf. Tob 14:5). The house that God rebuilds does not neglect the dead of Israel. Tobit's eschatological hopes include not only the aspect of time in terms of its fullness but also the dimension of space in terms of the return of all of Israel to the land. The desire for burial in the land as an ancestral holding begins, and looks forward to, the realization of such a claim. God's mercy will, of course, actualize the eschatological hopes both in its temporal and spatial dimensions.

Tobit's burial of the Jewish victims of Sennacherib recalls an episode from the life of David,[37] whom Tobit considers his ancestor/father (GII 1:4). For a northerner, Tobit's loyalty to the house of David is exemplary. As recounted in 2 Samuel 21, David hands over to the Gibeonites the seven sons of Saul except for Mephibosheth to be put to death as recompense. Once the sons are killed, Rizpah, the mother of the two of the sons, guards and keeps vigil to protect the bodies from birds and wild animals. Her action shames David, moving him to retrieve and gather the bones of Saul and his son Jonathan from the citizens of Jabesh-Gilead. David brings their bones for proper burial into the family tomb in their own land. Apparently, this moves God to grant mercy and relieve the land of famine. If this practice of burial connects Tobit to David and to the history of his people, does Tobit then bury the dead in the hopes of receiving a similarly land-related response from God?

---

36. Beyerle ("Release Me," 85) claims that "the eschatology in Tobit 13–14 has not only a "horizontal" orientation, in terms of an awareness of things that will happen in the future, but also a spatial dimension."

37. See Schüngel-Straumann, *Tobit*, 63.

ENDOGAMY AND THE INHERITANCE OF THE LAND

The spatial dimension of the eschatology embraced in the narrative is, in fact, hinted at in Tobit's instruction in which he commands his son to make a proper marriage by way of endogamy as his ancestors once did (Tob 4:12):

> First of all, marry a woman from among the descendants of your ancestors; do not marry a foreign woman, who is not of your father's tribe; for we are the descendants of the prophets. Remember, my son, that Noah, Abraham, Isaac, and Jacob, our ancestors of old, all took wives from among their kindred. They were blessed in their children, and their posterity will inherit the land.

One major reason that Tobit provides to persuade his son to practice endogamy has to do with the inheritance of the land. If Tobiah takes a wife from his own kin, he can expect his children to partake of that inheritance. For George Nickelsburg, the relevance of endogamy in a narrative set in the Diaspora lies in its sociopsychological factors; as a member of the minority group in a foreign environment, to marry within the dominant culture may be viewed as a sign of scornful disdain of one's own group which can consequently lead to the disintegration of the nation and to religious disorder and cultural chaos.[38] A related socio-cultural factor is the fear that by marrying foreigners, Jews would disappear into Gentile society.[39] In the end, however, such reasons pale in comparison to those associated with the land.

The practice of endogamy certainly exemplifies and reinforces the importance of kinship, a paramount concern of the story. The dynamic of kinship helps ensure the established continuity of land possession. The preference for an in-group marriage or marriage within a prescribed circle of kin has to do, therefore, with the economic and agrarian need for a man, whose multigenerational connection to the land is the avenue through which the household survives, to have a wife from kin whose highly specific local knowledge is useful and necessary for managing a land-based economy.[40] In agrarian societies, marriage within kin is preferred for its economic advantages. Of course, having worked in the royal court, Tobit's

---

38. See Nickelsburg, "Tobit," 796. See also Miller, *Marriage*, 79–82.

39. See Otzen, *Tobit and Judith*, 37. See also Pitkänen, "Family Life," 107–8; 113–15.

40. See Meyers, *Discovering Eve*, 185–86: "In agrarian setting, the closer the families of bride and groom, the more likely the bride would have learned the techniques of household labor that would best serve the new household" (185).

world is not necessarily agrarian. Superseding other possible motivations, the discourse prefers the inheritance of the land as the reason why Tobiah is to choose endogamy. Endogamy as a practice shows faith regarding the inheritance of the land. The linking of endogamy to the inheritance of the land envelops the custom with an eschatological aura.

Endogamy takes place in the narrative after Asmodeus is banished to Egypt.[41] The endogamous marriage of Tobiah and Sarah serves as pivot point or the nerve center of the narrative. It symbolizes then a new stage in which God acts anew and now begins to accomplish his creative purposes. The marriage of Tobiah and Sarah becomes a sign of God's desire and unwavering commitment to fulfill his word in the near future as he once did in the patriarchal past. The seven children from this union referred to in Tob 14:3 may in fact represent a new society,[42] or at the very least, "a new line that will continue and grow."[43] Thus, the marriage of Tobiah and Sarah may denote the creation of a new and restored household of Israel, with "Tobiah and Sarah as founders" just as Abraham and Sarah were for Israel.[44] The fruitfulness of this marriage provides Tobit the continuation of his lineage, a sign that indeed God will be true to his word even after his death. Re-enacting the history of their ancestors who married within their kinship circle, the endogamous marriage of Tobiah and Sarah provides a hint, if only a glimpse into the eschatological reality in which the house of Israel is restored to the land in order to continue its tenure there. The marriage of Tobiah and Sarah "carries forward the hope of a return to the "land of Abraham" (Tob 14:7)."[45] As Tobit has promised, the posterity of those who practice endogamy will inherit the land. The land, of course, completes this biblical complex, since the land binds all of Israel together in familial kinship not only in life but also in death.

Interestingly, the two essential commands in the Book of Tobit are endogamy and almsgiving with burial of the dead as its paradigmatic manifestation; both commands are unique in that they make claims that go beyond what is stipulated in the Book of Moses although they are presented

---

41. For Ego, "The Book of Tobit and the Diaspora," 51, Asmodeus represents the ideal negation of endogamy.

42. Nowell, "The Book of Tobit," 1026.

43. Miller, *Marriage*, 151.

44. See ibid., 148.

45. Nowell, "An Ancestral Story," 4.

as normative according to the Mosaic Torah.[46] One other element that both practices share is their association with land possession. Endogamy is intimately tied to the inheritance of the land while the practice of burying the dead is related to Israel's tenure in the land. Additionally, Tobit views the proper burial of parents after their deaths a significant aspect of complying with the divine commandment to honor parents which Deuteronomy intimately associates with existence in the land (cf. Deut 5:16). In this regard, both the practices of endogamy and the performance of burial acquire an eschatological color in terms of spatial dimension. In the view of the story, burial and endogamy are crucial because they are practices that not only look forward to but also make present the future reality of the full inheritance of the land. If the return of the dispersed Jews to their homeland is indeed one of the author's principal goals in telling the story,[47] the emphasis on burial and endogamy may be the human means that claim, prepare, and anticipate such a restoration and return to the land.

CONCLUDING REMARKS

In the worldview of the story, the practice of burial in the Book of Tobit speaks to the importance of kinship and family relations. Since all of Israel is kin, the dead of Israel are to be provided burial at the very least. Tobit's entombment of his righteous co-religionists may be viewed as a symbolic incorporation of those who die outside the land into the household of Israel. To bury the exiled dead is to gather them back with the ancestors; they are restored by burial to the family of Jacob. More importantly, burial of the dead is related to the land holdings of the family. Burial serves as a marker of family territory. The practice of burial as a land-related activity is paired with the narrative preference for endogamy, the primary motivation for which is land inheritance. Burial and endogamy are the recommended practices in the story that pertain to land claims. The activities of burial and endogamy, therefore, exude an eschatological orientation.

Tobit's seemingly simple instruction for a proper burial upon his death may be assuming a complex of ideas. Although it is conjectural, it is nevertheless plausible that Tobit may have expected the final interment of his mortal remains in the land of Israel, where his family grave would have been located. Following the precedents set by Jacob and Joseph in Genesis,

---

46. See Macatangay, "Wisdom Discourse of Tobit," 99–111.

47. See Bauckham, "Tobit as a Parable," 159.

a book that is often cited as shaping the crafting of the narrative, Tobit may have expected his descendants to take care of his bones when God finally remembers, visits, and fulfills his promise of land to Israel. The practice of secondary burial may also lie behind Tobit's instruction for burial with the necessary rites. If this custom is the case, then Tobit considers the land of Israel as the family grave writ large for the members of the household of Jacob. In this way, the dead will truly mark the land on behalf not only of the living but more importantly on behalf of all those future descendants and remnants of the scattered dead who will continue their line (cf. 14:5). This certainly speaks to the narrative claims on the land, which God in his great act of mercy, will realize for all of Israel when the appointed time comes. God's rebuilding of his house includes the dead of Israel. In the end, the promise of life from death has to do with Israel's resettlement in and re-possession of the land and this divine promise encompasses and holds for both the living and the dead of the house of Israel.

5

Almsgiving and the Restoration of Israel

In the end, the Book of Tobit grounds its hope that Israel will live again in the land in Tobit's experience of God's care. As one of the most prominent theological emphases of the story, Tobit's affirmation of divine providence posits a good and wisely ordered world in which every deficit finds its corresponding sufficiency and every want contains a beginning of another's fulfillment.[1] Amidst the chaos and anxiety of life in exile, God exercises firm control albeit in ways that are often mysterious. In short, God continues to provide for his people and his creative intention still holds in the dispersion despite appearances to the contrary.

In this context, burial of the dead can be seen as a narrative catalyst that exposes God's unremitting and active care upon those who die away from the land. Biblically, the friends of God who die within his blessings, like Abraham, Sarah, and Jacob, receive proper interment. To receive entombment is a fundamental sign that God has graced such a life and to be denied proper funerary rites is to suffer the fate of the wicked. That Tobit provides burial for his righteous fellow Jews implies that those who have died outside the land but receive burial do not die outside of God's purview; they may be far from the land but not far from God's providential gaze. Burial shows that even in exile the dead enjoy a relationship with the God of life who will ultimately deliver on his outstanding promises to his people.

1. Schellenberg, "Suspense," 313–27.

In a way, the dispersed dead are also like Moses, whom God buried before Israel entered the Promised Land. Since Moses was buried in a place of transition and at a "crossing point" to the land,[2] those whom Tobit buried outside the land are also on a threshold with a view of the possibility of having the divine promise of land fulfilled in their descendants. In certain ways, to be buried is to be in transition. Burial while in exile then is like a flicker in the darkness on the promising resolution to the great divide between God's providential purpose for his people and their situation of dispersion. This final chapter looks at how Tobit's burial of the dead as an act of mercy relates and looks forward to God's merciful action of restoring Israel to life in the land.

THE DEATH OF TOBIT

The story of Tobit concludes with a telling report on his death, according to which, Tobit died in peace at the age of one hundred and twelve (14:2). Since he was sixty-two years of age when he lost his vision (in GI, his age is fifty-eight), Tobit's life span was clearly longer than he earlier expected or imagined, having thought that he would die before reaching a ripe old age after asking God for death in prayer (4:2). His long years and peaceful death show a divinely approved life. The story quickly adds that he lived in wealth and prosperity after recovering his sight. His grandchildren also surrounded Tobit at the violet hour of his life (14:2). This last detail is critical in the context of lineage and family and in a worldview that constructs personal identity in social and corporate terms.[3] As one inextricably bound with family, death is not Tobit's end but life as is evident in his continuing progeny and legacy. From an Old Testament perspective, at least, the perpetuation of the family line, the number, and the survival of children are topmost blessings. To enjoy longevity and to see one's extended family gathered around at one's deathbed all point to a blissful existence.[4] And so, these summary announcements are remarkably instructive for they point to a life that has been positively and truly satisfied by God (12:9).

The narrative assessment of Tobit's death echoes that of Abraham's. As part of the divine promises, God assures Abraham in a vision that he will go to his ancestors in peace and be buried in a good old age (Gen 15:15).

---

2. See Stavrakopoulou, *Land of our Fathers*, 55–80.

3. See De Vito, "Construction of Personal Identity," 221–25.

4. See Anderson, "Tobit as Righteous Sufferer," 500–501.

The promise is later fulfilled when Gen 25:7 reports that Abraham died contented at a ripe old age, buried by his two sons Isaac and Ishmael in the family grave. Tobit's death also recalls that of Job's who died "old and contented" (Job 42:17).[5] With similar notices, Tobit can be included in this company of the beatified.[6] If the deaths of Abraham, Job, and Tobit mean that they end up going down to Sheol to endure its gloomy agonies as their inevitable fate, then the happy ending of their stories would be spurious. That the dank and dreary darkness of the netherworld is not the ultimate destiny of the blessed is perhaps the best way to make sense of the narrative estimation of Tobit's end. Instead of going to the abode of the dead, as he earlier requested in prayer, Tobit lives and dies blessed. In Tobit's case as in Job's, death is not an extension of an unfortunate life; death does not prolong Tobit's experience of darkness. Tobit's walk among the dead and an existence without the light of heaven are not made permanent by death. Rather, death closes a life that overflows with divine favors including a guaranteed progeny. Such is the case that even in death, there is so much life around him.

It is perhaps unavoidable to relate here Tobit's moment of death with his earlier lament entreating God to send him into the abode of the dead, to continue to let him move among the dead bodies of Jewish victims in exile. Death does come for him, but not as he had sought—Tobit's death, to use the phrase of Jon D. Levenson, is a "fortunate death," fortunate indeed because Tobit does not end up in Sheol, the suitable realm for those who live incomplete and unfulfilled lives and whose lineage and family tree is cut off.[7] Death is naturally inevitable but Tobit's death does not negate God's abundant favors upon him. The narrative details that deal with his death provide the impression that he continues to enjoy a blessed relationship with God even in death, which would certainly be far from true if he were in the abode of the dead. God has taken Tobit back to life from the realm of darkness and this life in light, the story seems to imply, continues beyond the grave.

---

5. Portier-Young ("Eyes to the Blind," 14–27) explores the inter-textual connections between Job and Tobit.

6. Anderson ("Tobit as Righteous Sufferer," 501) argues for Tobit's inclusion in the list. See also Levenson, *Resurrection and the Restoration of Israel*, 79–81. "Whatever complaints one had against God could be properly relegated to the past, so long as God graced the end of one's life. This, and only this, could rob death of its sting" (169).

7. Levenson, *Resurrection and Restoration of Israel*, 67–81.

Tobit wins at death, dying fulfilled and in peace after a life full of days. Tobit's cornucopia of divine blessings points to the truth of Raphael's claim that almsgiving saves from darkness and those who give alms will enjoy a full life (Tob 12:9b). Tobit's life illustrates in the end that a life characterized by charity is rightly rewarded.[8] The description of Tobiah's life and his death makes it equally clear that the reward of a full life promised to the almsgiver extends beyond the life of the individual almsgiver and even spills over into the members of the household.

THE PARALLEL LIVES OF TOBIT AND ISRAEL

The narrative details regarding Tobit's death encapsulate the movement of Tobit's life and the implications of that particular life for the life of Israel as a nation. To be sure, Tobit is a corporate figure that represents the collective, a character that stands in for the nation of Israel.[9] His experience of suffering, death, and life is not merely personal or individual but social and national.[10] Tobit's life thus corresponds to that of Israel's, and what happens to Tobit can be expected to happen to Israel.

Tobit's life story then not only recapitulates but also anticipates the historical movements in the life of Israel; the vicissitudes of his life parallel and embody the historical experience of the nation. The restoration of his sight, the return of his son, and Tobiah's fruitful marriage to Sarah are all a piece of God's providential intervention and covenant blessings of life in the present. In the land of exilic darkness, God is actually near, mysteriously involved in the lives of Tobit and his family. God's life-giving blessings have accompanied Tobit even in exile. Tobit's life manifests, therefore, God's favor and action of raising him from the great abyss (13:2), from an

---

8. Anderson, ("Tobit as Righteous Sufferer," 499) notes the irony involved in Tobit's last words to his son when he told him that "almsgiving delivers from death" (4:10), "for Tobit made this gnomic assertion against the background of his own personal despair. In the context of his life up to that point, it would have been more accurate to say that almsgiving had been the cause of death!"

9. See Nickelsburg, "Tobit," 719; Ego, "The Book of Tobit and the Diaspora," 45; Dancy, *The Shorter Books of the Apocrypha*, 5; Davies, "Didactic Stories," 100.

10. Levenson (*Resurrection and the Restoration of Israel*, 154–55), in discussing the typical biblical stories about widowhood and remarriage, infertility and birth, and return of vanished children, argues that these are "*social* in character and could not, therefore, be disengaged from the historical fate of the subjects of whom they were predicated" (154; emphasis his).

exilic existence as undesirable and miserable as Sheol, providing the prospect that Israel will not stay forever in the realm of the dead. Tobit's present experience of restoration into life shows that the kernel of such prophetic expectations and eschatological hopes for Israel have already started to be fulfilled.[11] Just as God has brought Tobit up from the world of the dead, so too it is hoped that God would bring Israel back from exile into their ancestral land.

Such hopes for deliverance from death ultimately arise from the belief that God is powerful over the realm of the dead. Victorious over the primordial darkness and chaotic waters of creation, the providential God can be relied upon to rescue from the clutches of death those who are perishing, including and especially Israel, his firstborn son. This is, of course, where the narrative holds the tension between the personal story of Tobit and the national story of Israel.[12] For Tobit, being raised to life is a present reality while the restoration for Israel remains only a glimmer of hope. This is why Raphael advises Tobit to bless and acknowledge God for all the good things God has done for him (12:6). The rationale behind the advice for public praise and witness[13] seems to be that Tobit's experience of resurrection can inspire and build up the faith of Israel as a nation, that Tobit's experience of being raised to life is also what God has in store for his people. And so, Tobit sings a song of thanksgiving emphasizing what God intends to do for his people based on his own personal experience (13:1–17). Tobit recognizes that God's marvelous and saving act of mercy brims over and extends beyond the confines of his own personal life into the life of Israel as a nation. God's merciful acts for Tobit and his family offer a foretaste of God's salvific activity for Israel.

Before dying and surrounded by his son and his grandchildren, Tobit predicts the restoration of Israel. Since identity is embedded in the family and the tribe, there is a sense in which Tobit will also survive exile no matter how long it takes and that he will see the realization of his own prediction and the fulfillment of God's promise of land when his family and his future descendants, viewed as the new household of Israel, continue to endure.[14] If

---

11. Hicks-Keeton, "Already/Not Yet," 97–117, notes the tension between God's present activity of fulfilling prophetic hopes for the future and the as-yet unrealized eschatological hopes.

12. For this analysis, see Anderson, "Tobit as Righteous Sufferer," 503, who also notes that this may be the reason for the composition of the story.

13. See also Estes, "Place of the Gentiles," 80–83.

14. On this, see Levenson, *Resurrection and Restoration of Israel*, 118, 170.

Tobit's prediction of a bright future after affliction happens to his children and descendants, then this would be proof enough of God's fidelity to his covenant word as given voice by the prophets of Israel (cf. 14:4). No wonder Tobit can proudly exclaim how happy and blessed he will be if a remnant of his descendants should survive and see the rebuilding of Jerusalem, the manifestation of God's glory (13:16). Since Tobit has experienced blessing and progeny before his death, he is sure that the inheritance of land as the last item of God's covenant promises will soon come to him and the dispersed household of Jacob.

TOBIT'S ALMSGIVING AND GOD'S MERCY

Inserted within the positive indications of God's copious blessings upon Tobit at his death is a reference to certain dispositions or behavioral actions that have defined his life, namely almsgiving and the acknowledgement of God's wonders (Tob 14:2). This is not incidental in the least. Divine blessings are typically associated with a proper relationship with God. In the narrative, the proper relationship that Tobit has with God and that all of Israel is encouraged to have is defined in terms of almsgiving; acts of charity function as the paradigm for what it means to walk in truth and in righteousness. To engage in almsgiving is to observe the Torah; it is to remember God. Almsgiving is presented in fact as "the sum of all the commandments."[15] In other words, to give alms is to enliven and activate the relationship with God.

The narrative insists that Tobit is an indefatigable almsgiver, even assuming great personal risks to fulfill the dictates of charity. In exile, Tobit fulfills the demands of righteousness by performing works of mercy. His story shows that his righteousness, his fidelity to God, and his observance of the divine commands by way of almsgiving is unquestionable. His story proves that those who remain close and loyal to the God of life even while in darkness can expect to live, prosper, and flourish. As Tobit notes in his instruction to Tobiah, those who act in truth, or those who practice righteousness by almsgiving, will truly prosper (4:6). Tobit's experiences of being restored to an abundant life show his own statements (4:11) and Raphael's promise (12:9) on behalf of almsgiving and acts of charity to be reliable and true.

15. Anderson, *Charity*, 107.

The personal catastrophes of the main characters as recounted in the Book of Tobit exude an aura of irreversibility. No doctor was able to heal Tobit's blindness. Sarah's husbands all died before consummating the marriage because of an irrational and jealous demon, against whom no earthly power would be able to prevail. That there are seven husbands dead in the hands of Asmodeus proves that all possibilities for marriage have been extinguished or exhausted. Since their afflictions look insurmountable, both Tobit and Sarah are resigned to their destinies. If their fates were to be upturned, it would have to happen by a special intervention. In a response to their prayers, the reader indeed learns very early on that such a reversal of misfortune will take place by divine fiat—Raphael is sent to heal Tobit of his blindness and Sarah will be bound to Tobiah in marriage (3:17).[16] For the blind Tobit to recover his sight and for desperate Sarah to have a husband and for both to enjoy the unexpected blessing of issue and posterity can only be God's work, from whom such astonishing reversals can be expected. In short, God in his righteous will has intervened to transform their irremediable situation of death into life, a sign that God will also intervene to overturn the situation of Israel's alienation from the land of promise.

The favorable turn of events on the wedding night of Tobiah and Sarah are ascribed to God's mercy. Tobiah was expected to suffer the same fate of death as Sarah's seven previous husbands with a grave already dug for his burial. It turns out that Tobiah is alive. In the logic of the prayers said before and after the marriage, their well-being and marriage are due to God's mercy. After Raguel has decided to give his daughter Sarah to Tobiah, he ends his words to Tobiah with a prayer asking the Lord of Heaven to grant him mercy and peace (7:11 GII). On their wedding night, Tobiah invites Sarah to beg the Lord for mercy and salvation (8:5). When later Raguel finds out that Tobiah is alive, he bursts into praise, acknowledging that God has shown mercy toward his only two children (8:15–17). In fact, his brief prayer overflows with four references to God's mercy! And so, Tobiah's virtual exodus from grave to life is owed to God's mercy. It is the selfsame mercy that will account for dispersed Israel's passage from death to life.

The restoration of Tobit's eyesight elicits a prayer of thanksgiving in which Tobit praises God for raising him from the dead. His prayer is couched in the language of divine affliction and mercy (11:14–15). In his joyful hymn in Tobit 13, Tobit praises the God who scourges and who has mercy, who casts down to the depths of the netherworld and who brings up

---

16. See Macatangay, "Apocalypticism and Narration," 207–20.

from the great abyss. The praise recalls Tobit's earlier claim in his discourse that "the Lord raises whomever he chooses to raise and casts down whomever he chooses to cast down" (4:19). After Tobit sings his own personal praises using the very same language he employed to describe his experience of healing, he directs the Israelites to praise and exalt God before the Gentiles. Tobit tells them that God has scourged them for their iniquities but will again have mercy on them; he will gather them from all the Gentiles among whom they have been scattered. This hymn of praise in Tobit 13 makes evident the tight narrative link between the events that transpired in Tobit's exilic life and the future restoration of all scattered Israel. His personal praise after his healing, which he repeats later in his hymn, and his direct exhortation to the Israelites are parallel, showing that the story of Tobit is analogous to the story of Israel. "To have mercy" describes God's restorative work for Tobit and Israel.

> "Though he afflicted me, he has had mercy on me. Now I see my son Tobiah." (11:15)

> "For he afflicts and he shows mercy; he leads down to Hades in the lowest regions of the earth and he brings up from the great abyss." (13:3)

> "He will afflict you for your iniquities but will again show mercy on all of you. He will gather you from all the nations among whom you have been scattered." (13:5)

In light of Tobit's healing, the casting down to the depths of Hades is not the biological cessation of life and the bringing up from the great abyss is not a resurrected personal life. At the end of the story, Tobit is described as enjoying the fullness of life surrounded with children and grandchildren; he is restored to health and enjoys prosperity to a happy old age—this is what it means to be "raised from the dead." In this parallelism, Tobit's blindness is an experience of the depths of the netherworld; it is God's scourge. Tobit's restoration of sight and life is an experience of being brought up from the great abyss: it is God's mercy. The personal lot of Tobit parallels the national fate of Israel and a similar movement will be valid for exiled Israel. God scourged the Israelites for their iniquities by scattering them, an experience of being cast down. And yet, God will again raise Israel from the abyss and grant them abundant life in the land, an experience and sign of God's mercy. The God who brought Tobit up from the realm of the dead and raised him to life can do the same for Israel, grounding thus Israel's hope for restoration.[17] And so, if the God of life can restore Tobit's sight and furnish Sarah with a husband and thus the possibility of a family, if God can raise them up, then surely God can revive Israel and restore them to the land. Like Tobit—to use again the words of Jon Levenson—"no one who knows God and has experienced the fulfillment of his promise, it would seem, is dead."[18]

The reversals of the seemingly unalterable fates of Tobit and Sarah function as parallels to the reversal of Israel's circumstance of exile into restoration. The story suggests that the key to the reversal of the condition of Tobit lies in his observance of almsgiving and mercy. In a similar way, if exiled Israel engages in almsgiving as a way to keep fidelity with God while away from the land, the inversion of their exilic condition can be expected. Tobit's instruction to Israel in his canticle makes this evident. Resounding the prophetic call to turn back to God, Tobit directs Israel to do what is true before God (13:6). Of course, the story has already made clear that the Semitic phrase "to do what is true" or "to act in truth" means to practice righteousness and to engage in almsgiving and works of mercy. The key that opens up the possibility of reversal lies in the righteous relationship of Israel with God defined in terms of almsgiving and mercy. Almsgiving and mercy is how Israel pursues righteousness and draws near to God while in exile in order to experience life.

To appreciate this point, it might be helpful to turn to Jon Levenson's discussion of the image of the Divine Warrior and Israel's adaptation of the Canaanite myth of Baal as they pertain to the biblical language of death and resurrection, noting that the advent and presence of God brings about the deliverance that intimately ties together created nature and the history of God's people—nature is revitalized and his people flourish in God's presence. This reality is indicative of the "new life that is a correlate of the renewed relationship between God and his people that human repentance and divine grace conjointly bring about . . . the normal state of affairs when the people of Israel are faithful to the Lord's covenant with them."[19] Levenson further observes that "Israel's own fortunes dwindle and revive in relation to their distance from or nearness to him. . .when they are distant from him, or he from them, they sicken and perish. When they re-approach him in repentance, or he returns to them in deliverance, they

---

17. Anderson, "Did Jesus Confess His Sins?," 464–65.

18. Levenson, *Resurrection and the Restoration of Israel*, 162.

19. Ibid., 214.

revive and flourish."[20] For Tobit, to return to God is to do what is true and to practice righteousness and mercy.

The pivot around which the deliverance and restoration of Israel revolves is a relationship that is defined in terms of almsgiving and mercy. When Israel does what is true, God will no longer hide his face from them, God will look with favor upon them and show them his mercy (13:6; cf. 4:7). Like Tobit, Israel can also be delivered from darkness and death in order to enjoy the abundance of life in the land if it returns to God by way of almsgiving and mercy while away from the land. It is therefore no accident that Tobit's dying words to his son and grandchildren emphasize the need to live a life exemplified by charity: "So now my children, I command you, serve God faithfully and do what is pleasing in his sight. Your children are also to be commanded to do what is right and to give alms, and to be mindful of God at all times with sincerity and with all their strength" (14:8–9). Almsgiving is how Israel enacts, embodies, and expresses faith in the goodness of the God of life and his promises.[21]

The gathering in the land of those who have been scattered is due ultimately to God's mercy (13:6) in the same way that Tobit's restoration of sight comes from God's mercy (11:15). God's mercy is the common element active in bringing Tobit, and later righteous Israel, to life. If mercy defines God's righteous relationship with Tobit, then God's righteous relationship with Israel will be revealed equally as mercy. Divine mercy is responsible for the movement from death to life in the case of Tobit, as it will later be in the case of righteous Israel. Life in full is life in the land. God's mercy will make it possible for the divine purpose and the historical event to forge as one again.

THE "ADEQUATE REWARD"

No one can cast doubt that Tobit conducts a righteous life by giving alms and engaging in works of mercy. To an even greater extent, no one can doubt that God is righteous. God's righteousness will be shown in his merciful act of restoring Israel to the land. Moreover, the story gives the impression that God's righteousness matches Tobit's righteousness. If Tobit can risk so much in behaving righteously by way of mercy and almsgiving, would God

20. Ibid., 215.

21. See Anderson, "Almsgiving as an Expression of Faith," 121–31: "[T]he practice of giving alms directly correlates to the experience or disposition of faith."

not respond with a corresponding and reciprocal righteousness by way of his mercy? This parallel interplay between God's righteousness and Tobit's righteousness is evident in the way the story matches the important adjectives used of Tobit with those of God. In his prayer, Tobit describes God as righteous whose ways are mercy and truth (3:2), echoing God's self-revelation in Exod 34:6. In describing himself, Tobit declares with startling boldness that he has walked in the ways of truth and righteousness, performing acts of mercy all the days of his life (1:3). This observable correspondence between Tobit's and God's righteousness is a helpful hint in discerning the inner theological logic that binds and ultimately resolves the seeming tension between the personal story of Tobit and the national story of Israel.

To explore this underlying logic, it might be enlightening to borrow the idea of "an adequate reward," a reward that is adequate because it corresponds in quality to the behavior performed or the act done. Nils Alstrup Dahl explains this concept in terms of the principle of "measure for measure" as it applies to the binding of Isaac, also known as the Aqedah: that there is a parallelism between Abraham's conduct at the Aqedah and the conduct expected in return from God.[22] Tobit enunciates this principle in his discourse to his son when he tells Tobiah not to turn his face away from any of the poor so that God's face will not turn away from him (4:7). Tobit also gives voice to this principle in his song, reminding Israel that if they turn to God with all their heart and soul and do what is true before God, God will turn to them and will no longer hide his face from them (13:6). The principle of reciprocity connects human and divine actions.

Tobit's merciful deeds approximate and correspond with God's own. Tobit's act of mercy and almsgiving may then be viewed as a typological prefiguration of God's act of mercy. As recompense, God mimics what Tobit does. In other words, God would remember Tobit's act of mercy with a divine act of mercy as reward to the benefit of Israel in the same way that God rewarded Abraham's sacrifice by a corresponding action of offering his own son.

The patriarchal rendering of Tobit's character in the mold of Abraham may reinforce that this is the case in the Book of Tobit. For one thing, Tobit is like Abraham in that he is righteous and walks in the ways of God.[23] In

---

22. See Dahl, *The Crucified Messiah*, 148–53. Prof. Harry Nasuti directed me to this work when the paper was first presented at the *CBA* Meeting in Providence, Rhode Island.

23. Nowell ("An Ancestral Story," 4–5) notes the character similarities between Abraham and Tobit. See also Macatangay, *Wisdom Instructions*, 132; Perrin, "Tobit's Context

fact, the *Aqedah* may have served as a biblical model for part of the story. The sixth chapter of the narrative employs the phrase "the two of them went along together" and significantly uses the term "lad" or "young man" instead of referring specifically to the name of Tobiah: these details may all point to the crafting of the journey of Tobiah with Raphael disguised as a kin after the pattern of Genesis 22.[24] Like Abraham, Tobit undergoes a test. He risks his own son to uncover his commitment to charity. As a figure like Abraham, Tobit can expect God's action towards him to show some correspondence with his own towards God in the same way that God has acted towards Abraham. To be sure, Tobit is a representative figure but the narrative seems to endow him with more than a purely symbolic function—like Abraham, he is an individual whose actions determine, condition, and influence the existence of Israel.

This principle of "an adequate reward" in which God rewards Tobit's act of mercy with a similar or corresponding act of mercy helps resolve the tension between the two stories of Tobit and Israel. What Tobit has done for his people in exile by way of mercy and almsgiving, God will reward adequately by an act of mercy for Israel. In other words, Tobit's act of gathering the dead and providing them a place of burial in exile would elicit a corresponding divine action of gathering dead Israel and restoring them to live in the land. The prophet Ezekiel, of course, provides the most vivid picture of this divine act of bringing his people out of exile and restoring them to the land in his vision of the valley of the dry bones (Ezek 37:1–14).[25] To an extent, Tobit's burial of the dead in exile finds its visual counterpart in Ezekiel's vision in which God lifts Israel out of their graves by breathing on a vast multitude of desiccated bones in order to revive them. Ezekiel portrays in his vision what Tobit expects in return from God as an adequate reward for his acts of mercy.

The notion of remembrance also plays a part in showing reciprocity and correspondence between Tobit's and God's actions. Tobit remembers

---

and Contacts," 31–32.

24. See Novick, "Biblicized Narrative," 755–64. See also Anderson, *Charity*, 90–96.

25. See Levenson, *Resurrection and the Restoration of Israel*, 156–65. Ezekiel's vision of Israel's renewal and restoration involves a spiritual and moral transformation owing to "God's prevenient action" of replacing Israel's "heart of stone" with a "heart of flesh." In the Book of Tobit, the moral transformation involves Israel's return to the ways of righteousness. Tobit limits his works of charity to those who are righteous and mindful of God. In his hymn, Tobit instructs Israel to turn to the Lord and do what is right before him and perhaps God may look with favor upon Israel and show them his mercy (13:6).

God by observing the law while in exile and as a result, God has given him the favor of a good standing in the court of Shalmaneser (1:10). Of course, Tobit displays his mindfulness of God by almsgiving and charity. In his prayer, Tobit asks the Lord to remember him (3:3). This plea for remembrance recalls the record of God's marvelous involvement and providential acts in the history of his people.[26] In this regard, there is a sense that God will satisfy Tobit's act of remembrance with God's own remembrance of Tobit. Tobit's restoration of sight and Tobiah's marriage to Sarah confirm such divine remembrance. If Israel remembers God by practicing righteousness, Israel will also experience God's gracious remembrance.

The balanced literary structure of the story further contributes to the impression that God will reward Tobit's mercy with an act of mercy for Israel. The first two and the last two chapters mention truth, righteousness, and mercy; these concepts frame the story. At the beginning of the story, Tobit claims to have the foremost qualities of truth, righteousness and mercy, certainly attributes that reside in God's self-revelation. These qualities will echo again at the end of the story as Tobit gives a farewell testament instructing his son and his seven grandchildren to serve God in truth and to practice righteousness and mercy. As he lays dying, Tobit predicts that those who are mindful of God, that is, those who practice truth, righteousness and mercy, will come to Jerusalem in security and dwell in the land of Abraham forever (14:7). The first narrative frame abounds with references to burial of the dead while the second frame teems with references to restoration and ingathering. This literary structuring gives the impression that Tobit's activity and preoccupation with burial of kin in the beginning of the narrative corresponds as well as gives way to the restoration of Israel envisioned at the end of the story. Tobit's burial of the dead and God's renewal of Israel correspond in that they are both described as acts of mercy. The story posits reciprocity of mercy between God and Tobit.

One of the questions the narrative poses with the mention of the testing in Tobit 12 is whether Tobit will remain steadfast in his convictions regarding charity. That Tobit sends his only son on a perilous journey to retrieve a good sum of money so that Tobiah can be an almsgiver like him is proof that Tobit embraces the truth of his commitments. If Tobit's fidelity to God is shown in his acts of mercy despite the testing, the question becomes: will God's fidelity and commitment to his people be demonstrated

26. See Ego, "The Book of Tobit and the Diaspora," 47–48; Macatangay, "Acts of Charity," 72–80.

even more clearly through his act of kindness toward them? If Tobit buries and gathers the dead of his kin despite the ridicule and the personal perils, would God not do whatever it takes to gather and restore his people to life in the land? While Tobit's fidelity to God and belief in the salvific value of mercy requires testing, God's fidelity to his people and his steadfast kindness and loving mercy do not.

Tobit's charitable action of gathering the scattered dead of his kin looks forward to God's charitable action of restoring the disintegrating house of Israel. Tobit's act of burying the dead, which particularizes mercy, has its narrative counterpart in God's regeneration and renewal of Israel, which concretizes the divine act of mercy. God's mercy for Tobit lies in the healing of his deathlike condition of blindness just as God's mercy for Israel will later manifest in the healing of Israel's situation of decay and death. The seeds of hope for the restoration of dead Israel, which the story anticipates, are already planted in the beginning as the story introduces Tobit's act of burial while in exile. Put differently, Tobit's merciful action of gathering and burying the dead heralds God's future merciful action of gathering and restoring the house of Israel in the land of promise.

CONCLUDING REMARKS

The details that attend Tobit's death at the end of the narrative are not trivial. That the story takes pains to describe the kind of life Tobit has lived at the dusk of his life attests to the importance of portraying a life deemed to have been completely blessed by God. In his relationship with the God of life, Tobit's experience of death does not have the final word on his life. His experience of darkness does not extend into and beyond the grave. Rather, the abundance of God's graces counters the physical inevitability of death. If Tobit as a character represents the nation of Israel and if the stories of Tobit and Israel run parallel, then it is likely that righteous Israel's fate of death in the dispersion would also end in life, that is, life in the land. God's remembrance of Tobit while walking among the dead serves as a pointer to such a possibility for Israel.

Divine blessings in Tobit's life flow out of his active and faithful relationship with God. Tobit's continued service and fidelity to God by way of almsgiving and acts of mercy results in life. His almsgiving shows his belief in the goodness of God. Tobit exhorts Israel to engage in charity and almsgiving as a way to remember God and to maintain a righteous relationship with him. If Israel shows its faith in God in this way while away from the land, Israel can expect to be raised from the dead just as Tobit has experienced this in his life. God reciprocates and matches Tobit's act of mercy with his very own mercy. The story posits a dynamic interplay between God's righteous response and Israel's responsibility of righteous behavior as God's elect. And so, if Israel engages in acts of mercy, the people can also expect a corresponding act of mercy from God.

The primacy of mercy characterizes divine providence in favor of Tobit and Israel. God rewards Tobit's act of mercy adequately with his own divine mercy and Israel can anticipate the same if they too act with mercy in service to God. Of course, Tobit's mercy finds its paradigmatic manifestation in his practice of burying the dead. The burial of the dead comprises Tobit's act of mercy while the gathering and restoration of Israel in the land defines God's. In the end, Tobit's merciful act of gathering the dispersed dead of Israel will find a corresponding action from the God who will gather the bones of dead Israel into the land in order to quicken them into life. Just as Tobit shows his fidelity to God before the nations by way of almsgiving and other acts of mercy, so too God will show his faithfulness to his chosen people before all the nations by way of his own marvelously merciful work of restoring Israel to the land of promise to enjoy abundant life there.

Epilogue

TOBIT AND SAUL

THE HUNGARIAN FILM *Son of Saul* directed by László Nemes won rave reviews and cinematic awards worldwide, including the 2015 Grand Prix de Jury at the Cannes Film Festival and the 2016 Best Foreign Language Film from the American Academy of Motion Picture Arts and Sciences. The narrative revolves around Saul Auslander, a Hungarian Jewish prisoner at the Auschwitz concentration camp who is a member of the camp's *Sonderkommandos* tasked with disposing the clothes and valuables of the Shoah victims before burning their corpses after they have died in the gas chambers. The movie portrays Saul's inner or subjective world—his impassivity, even indifference and business-like attitude to the horrors around him at first—in short, the film shows how Saul lost and later recovered his soul. From the moment that Saul witnesses a young boy briefly surviving the gas, only to be put to death a few minutes later by a Nazi doctor, Saul becomes consumed by the desire to salvage from anatomical dissection and from the incinerating flames the body of the boy he takes as his son, though the story remains unclear whether Saul really has a son. Able to feel again, and despite the odds, Saul commits to finding a Jewish rabbi in order to give the boy a proper Jewish burial.

Saul becomes a Knight of Faith, to use Soren Kierkegaard's lovely expression, a man who has found a mission, one who makes a commitment and pursues it with urgency and passion until the very end, as if it were the truest thing, even in the face of prodigious odds. Saul has become single-minded in his purpose. He is apathetic toward the revolt that his colleagues are planning against the Nazi commanders, regarding it as mere distraction from what he considers to be a far more essential and very personal search for a rabbi who can give the boy a suitable burial. His colleagues are bemused, even irritated by the attention Saul pays to one dead child in the midst of mass slaughter. They accused him of failing the living for the sake of the dead. But the commitment to give the boy a proper burial revives Saul, giving him a mission and purpose in his struggle to gain meaning in the midst of such desperate conditions. Saul may, as he says, "already be dead" but embracing this single cause gives meaning to his life.

This powerful film wants to impress upon the viewer that the recovery of the soul and the key to the proverbial meaning of life in the midst of hopeless and horrific circumstances lies in the virtues of taking care of others and assuming responsibility for others. When such virtues survive in places like Auschwitz, life finds some meaning. Perhaps, it is not a stretch to say then that Saul is a modern counterpart or rendition of Tobit. In exile, when it was thought that God had given up on his promises, when Israel as a nation was tending toward dissolution and decay, Tobit exercises care and charity for his fellow Jews in defiance of the odds that are stacked against him. Tobit shows his care of others most exceptionally by burying the dead. Like Saul, Tobit is unswerving in his dangerous pursuit of providing burial for his dead kin; he is a man on a mission even when fulfilling it seems almost impossible. Despite the personal risks, Tobit commits to charity and almsgiving as if they were the surest things. Like Saul, Tobit already feels dead in exile, but his consuming devotion to works of charity has given his life purpose; in fact, his commitment to almsgiving has brought him back to life.

For both Tobit and Saul, burial is a sacred task done for those who are kin. Saul takes the boy whose death he witnesses as his son and Tobit treats his fellow Israelites as kin. The commitment to burial in both narratives is in the context of fictive kinship. In the midst of chaos and death, the awareness that everyone is related awakens life. It is as though the experience of life is seldom primarily or entirely an individual affair. Life happens and grows in the interstices of interrelatedness. Life thrives in relationships. There is a difference, however, in the experiences of life between Saul and Tobit. For Saul, life is experienced in the present, for that is all he has. For Tobit, life is both a present and a future reality.

The search for a Jewish rabbi who can provide a proper burial for the dead boy rouses Saul to life and humanity while he remains immersed in a mechanized inferno. This desperate pursuit and solitary mission shows

Saul's determination to express his free will against such chaos ("I will" are the first words Saul says in the film), connecting him to something transcendent even if it were for a fleeting moment. Burying the dead has brought him life. In a similarly existential way, Tobit finds some purpose for life in exile in the practice of burying the bodies of the king's Jewish victims. Despite the challenges, Tobit inserts his will to continue believing in God expressed through his acts of charity and burial of the dead. For Tobit, such activities mean that his relationship with God has not ceased to exist; it means that he continues to enjoy a faithful relationship with God and that his exilic circumstances do not mean that God has abandoned him. It means, in the end, that through his works of charity, Tobit remains connected to the life-giving God despite glaring evidence to the contrary. And so, for Tobit and Saul, to bury the dead is to wage war against the forces of death; to bury the dead is to assert life. Burying the dead makes a paradoxical claim on the ideals of life in the midst of death.

Tobit's encounter with divine care has taught him that the God he trusts is a good God who is in the business of life; his God is a God who prevails over the overwhelming forces of death. Even in chaos, the beat of life pulses, indicating that God's power is not vanquished. The people of God are given the task of stoking the fire of life instead of snuffing it out. This responsibility can be done in many ways. For Tobit, almsgiving and other works of charity promote life in the midst of death. To show charity is to believe in the life that God offers. For when life-enhancing actions thwart decay and death, God responds with a reward of life.

TOBIT AND JESUS

In the Book of Tobit, life and grave are not opposites; they are in fact intimately entwined. Nowhere is this more evident than in the episode in which a grave is prepared and dug for Tobiah who is presumed to have died on the night of his wedding. The prepared grave is quickly covered and filled before daybreak upon finding out that Tobiah is well. The empty grave stands as a powerful testimony that the one who has been dismissed for dead is in fact alive. The empty grave shows that Tobiah has undergone a virtual exodus from death to life.

In this part of the Tobit story, at least, the sign of life is an empty tomb. This leaves one to wonder if the Book of Tobit helped provide the evangelists a fitting image and example for showing the credibility of the resurrection of Jesus, whose greatest act of charity is his self-gift, by way of an empty tomb. The burial of Jesus is an article of the Christian creed. In his first letter to the Corinthians, Saint Paul proclaims what is likely part of the earliest apostolic preaching—that Christ was buried, that he was raised on the third day in accordance with the scriptures, and that he appeared to the apostles and other early witnesses of the resurrection (cf. 1 Cor 15:3–8). In claiming that Jesus was buried, raised, and appeared, it is implied that the empty tomb is left behind. The sequence of events in Paul's kerygma suggests that in being raised from the dead, Jesus was raised from the grave, leaving his place of burial empty. Had the tomb not been empty, it would have been almost impossible for the apostles to proclaim the resurrection. Of course, the Jewish polemic that the disciples had stolen the body of Jesus at night (cf. Matt 28:11–15) is an attempt to explain away rather than deny the phenomenon of the empty grave of Jesus. The empty tomb demonstrates that the man who rose from the dead is the same man whose body was buried in that tomb.

No doubt, there are notable differences between the empty grave of Tobiah and that of Jesus. The empty grave of Tobiah is a fictional dramatization of the reality that Tobiah escaped his fate of death. Tobiah was actually never buried in the tomb. Tobiah's experience of death is figurative and only imminent. The grave intended specifically for Tobiah remained empty precisely because he was able to cheat death with angelic assistance. Tobit's beloved son, Tobiah, is symbolically restored to life with an empty grave as a sign. Jesus, on the other hand, did lie buried in the grave. His experience of death was real. The empty grave of Jesus is a historical reality that is a *sine qua non* for the resurrection. God's beloved son, Jesus, is literally raised to life with the empty tomb as a sign. Accordingly, the empty grave of Tobiah can be viewed in some ways as a typological prefiguration of the empty tomb of Jesus. That their graves are empty allows their burial, symbolic or otherwise, to stand in relation to life.

In Matthew's account of the resurrection, the women are said to have left the tomb with fear and great joy (cf. Matt 28:8). A tomb, of course, is not a place one comes away from with joy. In the early days of bereavement, one leaves the tomb in profound grief and sorrow and, later on, with a quiet resignation. Because the tomb is empty, however, the women can look to the future and find intimations of life there. In that comes their joy. In light of the Paschal event of Jesus, the empty tomb becomes a sign and an anticipation of the new exodus of God's people to a new Promised Land made possible by God's mercy.

TOBIT AND ISRAEL

The stories of Saul, Tobit, Israel, and Jesus emphatically declare that the grave does not necessarily point to death but to life. Indeed, it is a claim on the patrimony of life. For Israel, in particular, this patrimony of life includes the patrimony of the land.

Raguel's prayer of thanksgiving after finding out that Tobiah and Sarah are alive and well on their wedding night ascribes this surprising turn of events to God's mercy and compassion (8:17). Of course, it is also God's mercy and charity that will be responsible for the restoration of Israel in the land to enjoy abundance of life there. This episode, dramatically tied to a sense of a new beginning in the marriage of Tobias and Sarah, thus anticipates the exodus of dispersed Israel from the grave to life.

The death of the nation did not move the author of the Book of Tobit to write a eulogy for Israel. Instead, it has inspired the writer of the Book of Tobit to examine and distill the meaning of Israel's life as God's elect. For Tobit, Israel in exile is indeed dead and deserves burial. Like so many authors of his day, the writer of the Book of Tobit views the fact of the continued dispersion and decomposition of Israel as divine castigation for Israel's transgressions. Does this mean that Israel's life with God is over? The writer of the Book of Tobit gives an emphatic response in the negative. Tobit is a loyal member of God's elect whose activity of burying the dispersed dead of Israel attests to his charity and righteousness. There are still those faithful remnants that observe the commandments understood in the story in terms of charity and mercy. Tobit has not given up on his relationship with God, and while acknowledging the sovereignty of God, Tobit is sure that God has not given up on his people as his experience attests. Such fidelity fuels the hopes that Israel can still expect that exile is not God's decisive word on his relationship with Israel. God's covenant involves blessing, progeny, and inheritance of the land. Tobit's life shows the fulfillment of blessing and progeny, giving Tobit the confidence that possession of the land is forthcoming.

In the Book of Tobit, interment of the dead is neither only a corporal work of mercy nor merely a sign of respect and care for the dead. The practice of burying the dead has acquired a symbolic function derived from

Israelite complex of ideas regarding burial. To be sure, to bury the dead in the dispersion is to comply with the familial duty of burying the dead members of the house of Jacob. The interment of the mortal remains of Israel's dead is a critical action that is a responsibility incumbent upon Tobit as kin; the ethics of kinship demands it. In this way, interment reinforces collective identity and patrimonial claims. However, the collective fate of the dead of the family of Jacob is more than about reunion with the ancestors who, by burial, join the community of their kinship affiliation. Ultimately, it is about restoration to life in the land. Tobit's burial of the dead is a preparation for, and an acknowledgement of, the impending fulfillment of this prophetic expectation. His noble practice of burying his dead compatriots shines a spotlight on the possibility of life and rest in the land that dead Israel hopes to receive. By burying the dead of Israel, Tobit makes a claim that God's beloved son, Israel, will be raised to life. When the appointed time comes and when all the words of the prophets come true, God will restore and rebuild his house in the land of promise as God's spectacular showcase of mercy. That household happens to include all of Israel, both the dead and the living. In the end, the God of life gives life as his final word for those who show faith by acting in charity.

Bibliography

Abrahams, Israel. "Tobit and Genesis." *JQR* 5 (1892–1893) 348–50.

Albertz, Rainer. *Israel in Exile: The History and Literature of the Sixth Century B.C.E.* Translated by David Green. Studies in Biblical Literature 3. Atlanta: SBL, 2003.

Anderson, Gary A. "Almsgiving as an Expression of Faith." In *Emotions from Ben Sira to Paul*, edited by Renate Egger-Wenzel and Jeremy Corley, 121–32. Berlin: de Gruyter, 2012.

———. "The Book of Tobit and the Canonical Ordering of the Book of the Twelve." In *The Word Leaps the Gap: Essays on Scripture and Theology in Honor of Richard B. Hays*, edited by J. Ross Wagner et al., 67–75. Grand Rapids: Eerdmans, 2008.

———. *Charity: The Place of the Poor in the Biblical Tradition.* New Haven: Yale University Press, 2013.

———. "Did Jesus Confess His Sins at Baptism? Evidence from the Book of Tobit." In *Method and Meaning: Essays on New Testament Interpretation in Honor of Harold W. Attridge*, edited by Andrew B. McGowan and Kent H. Richards, 453–64. Resources for Biblical Study 67. Atlanta: SBL, 2011.

———. "Does Tobit Fear God for Nought." In *The Call of Abraham: Essays on the Election of Israel in Honor of Jon D. Levenson*, edited by Gary Anderson and Joel Kaminsky, 115–43. Christianity and Judaism in Antiquity 19. Notre Dame: University of Notre Dame Press, 2013.

———. "How Does Almsgiving Purge Sins?" In *Hebrew in the Second Temple Period: The Hebrew of the Dead Sea Scrolls and of Other Contemporary Sources. Proceedings of the Twelfth International Symposium of the Orion Center for the Study of the Dead Sea Scrolls and Associated Literature, Jointly Sponsored by the Eliezer Ben-Yehuda Center for the Study of the History of the Hebrew Language, 29–31 December 2008*, edited by Steven E. Fassberg et al., 1–14. Studies on the Texts of the Desert of Judah 108. Leiden: Brill, 2013.

———. "Sacrifice and Sacrificial Offerings (OT)." In *ABD* 5:870–86.

———. *Sin: A History.* New Haven: Yale University Press, 2009.

———. "Tobit as Righteous Sufferer." In *A Teacher for All Generations: Essays in Honor of James C. VanderKam*, edited by Eric Mason et al., 493–507. JSJSup 153. Leiden: Brill, 2011.

André, G. "פקד *pāqad.*" In *TDOT* 12:50–63.

Bailey, Lloyd R., Sr. *Biblical Perspectives on Death.* OBT. Philadelphia: Fortress, 1979.

Bauckham, Richard. "Tobit as a Parable for the Exiles of Northern Israel." In *Studies in the Book of Tobit: A Multidisciplinary Approach*, edited by Mark Bredin, 140–64. LSTS 55. London: T. & T. Clark, 2006.

Bertrand, Daniel A. "Un baton de vieillesse, a propos de Tobit 5,23 et 10,4 (Vulgate)." *RHPR* 71 (1991) 33–37.

Beyerle, Stefan. "Release Me to Go to My Everlasting Home . . . (Tob 3:6): A Belief in an Afterlife in Late Wisdom Literature." In *The Book of Tobit: Text, Tradition, Theology*, edited by Geza G. Xeravits and Jozsef Zsengeller, 71–88. JSJSup 98. Leiden: Brill, 2005.

Bloch-Smith, Elizabeth. "The Cult of the Dead in Judah: Interpreting the Material Remains." *JBL* 111 (1992) 213–24.

———. *Judahite Burial Practices and Beliefs about the Dead*. JSOTSup 123. Sheffield: Sheffield Academic, 1992.

Bolyki, Janos. "Burial as an Ethical Task in the Book of Tobit, in the Bible, and in the Greek Tragedies." In *The Book of Tobit: Text, Tradition, Theology*, edited by Geza G. Xeravits and Jozsef Zsengeller, 89–101. JSJSup 98. Leiden: Brill, 2005.

Brichto, Herbert C. "Kin, Cult, Land and Afterlife—A Biblical Complex." *HUCA* 44 (1973) 1–54.

Casson, Lionel. *Travel in the Ancient World*. Baltimore: Johns Hopkins University Press, 1994.

Collins, John J. *Between Athens and Jerusalem: Jewish Identity in the Hellenistic Diaspora*. New York: Crossroad, 1982.

———. "The Judaism in the Book of Tobit." In *The Book of Tobit: Text, Tradition, Theology*, edited by Geza G. Xeravits and Jozsef Zsengeller, 23–40. JSJSup 98. Leiden: Brill, 2005.

Corley, Jeremy. "Joseph as Exemplar of Wisdom: A Hidden Allusion in Sirach 21:11–21." In *The Temple in Text and Tradition: A Festschrift in Honor of Robert Hayward*, edited by R. Timothy McLay, 157–78. LSTS 83. London: Bloomsbury, 2015.

Cousland, J. Robert C. "Tobit: A Comedy in Error." *CBQ* 65 (2003) 535–53.

Craghan, John, C.SS.R. *Esther, Judith, Tobit, Jonah, Ruth*. OTM 16. Wilmington, DE: Glazier, 1982.

Crenshaw, James L. *Education in Ancient Israel: Across the Deadening Silence*. Anchor Bible Reference Library. New York: Doubleday, 1998.

Crouch, James E. *The Origin and Intention of the Colossian Haustafel*. Göttingen: Vandenhoeck & Ruprecht, 1972.

Dahl, Nils A. *The Crucified Messiah and Other Essays*. Minneapolis: Augsburg, 1974.

Dancy, J. C. *The Shorter Books of the Apocrypha: Tobit, Judith, Rest of Esther, Baruch, Letter of Jeremiah, Additions to Daniel and Prayer of Manasseh*. Cambridge Bible Commentary. Cambridge: Cambridge University Press, 1972.

Dávid, Nóra. "Burial in the Book of Tobit and in Qumran." In *The Dead Sea Scrolls in Context: Integrating the Dead Sea Scrolls in the Study of Ancient Texts, Languages, and Cultures*, edited by Armin Lange et al., 2:489–500. Vetus Testamentum Supplements 140. Leiden: Brill, 2011.

Davies, Philip R. "Didactic Stories." In *Justification and Variegated Nomism I: The Complexities of Second Temple Judaism*, edited by D. A. Carson et al., 99–133. Wissenschaftliche Untersuchungen zum Neuen Testament 2/140. Tübingen: Mohr/Siebeck, 2001.

Deselaers, Paul. *Das Buch Tobit: Studien zu seiner Entstehung, Komposition und Theologie.* OBO 43. Göttingen: Vandenhoeck & Ruprecht, 1982.

deSilva, David A. *Introducing the Apocrypha: Message, Context, and Significance.* Grand Rapids: Baker Academic, 2002.

De Vito, Robert A. "Old Testament Anthropology and the Construction of Personal Identity." *CBQ* (1999) 217–38.

Dimant, Devorah. "The Book of Tobit and the Qumran Halakhah." In *The Dynamics of Language and Exegesis at Qumran,* edited by Devorah Dimant and Reinhard G. Kratz, 121–43. Forschungen zum Alten Testament 2/35. Tübingen: Mohr/Siebeck, 2009.

———. "The Family of Tobit." In *With Wisdom as a Robe: Qumran and other Jewish Studies in Honor of Ida Fröhlich,* edited by Karoly Dobos and Miklos Koszeghy, 160–65. Sheffield: Sheffield Phoenix, 2008.

Di Pede, Elena, et al. *Révéler les oeuvres de Dieu. Lecture narrative du livre de Tobie.* Le livre et le rouleau 46. Namur: Lessius, 2014.

Efthimiadis-Keith, Helen. "The Significance of Food, Eating, Death and Burial in the Book of Tobit." *Journal for Semitics* 22 (2013) 553–78.

Ego, Beate. "The Book of Tobit and the Diaspora." In *The Book of Tobit: Text, Tradition, Theology,* edited by Geza G. Xeravits and Jozsef Zsengeller, 41–54. JSJSup 98. Leiden: Brill, 2005.

———. "Buch Tobit." In *Jüdische Schriften aus hellenistisch-römischer Zeit,* edited by Hermann Lichtenberger, 873–1007. Gütersloh: Gütersloher, 1999.

———. "Death and Burial in the Tobit Narration in the Context of the Old Testament Tradition." In *The Human Body in Death and Resurrection,* edited by Tobias Nicklas et al., 87–103. Deuterocanonical and Cognate Literature, Yearbook 2009. Berlin: de Gruyter, 2009.

———. "Denn er liebt sie (Tob 6:15 MS 319): Zur Rolle des Dämons Asmodäus in der Tobit-Erzählung." In *Die Dämonen: Die Dämonologie der israelitisch-jüdischen und frühchristlichen Literatur im Kontext ihrer Umwelt = Demons: The Demonology of Israelite-Jewish and Early Christian Literature in Context of their Environment,* edited by Armin Lange et al., 309–17. Tubingen: Mohr/Siebeck, 2003.

———. "Heimat in der Fremde: Zur Konstituierung einer Jüdischer Identität in Buch Tobit." In *Jüdische Schriften in ihren antik-jüdischen und urchristlichen Kontext,* edited by Hermann Lichtenberger and Gerbern S. Oegema, 270–83. Studien zu den Jüdischen Schriften aus hellenistisch-römischer Zeit 1. Gütersloh: Gütersloher, 2002.

———. "Tobits weisheitliches Vermächtnis (Tob 4)—Narratologische und theologische Aspekte." In *Weisheit als Lebensgrundlage: Festschrift für Friedrich V. Reiterer zum 65. Geburtstag,* edited by Renate Egger–Wenzel et al., 95–122. Deuterocanonical and Cognate Literature Studies 15. Berlin: de Gruyter, 2013.

Engel, Helmut. "Auf zuverlässigen Wegen und in Gerechtigkeit. Religiöses Ethos in der Diaspora nach dem Buch Tobit." In *Biblische Theologie und gesellschaftlicher Wandel: für Norbert Lohfink, SJ,* edited by Georg Braulik et al., 83–100. Freiburg: Herder, 1993.

Estes, Joel D. "The Place of Gentiles in the Book of Tobit." *BN* 166 (2015) 65–86.

Fassbeck, Gabriele. "Tobit's Religious Universe between Kinship Loyalty and the Law of Moses." *JSJ* 36 (2005) 173–96.

Fields, Weston W. "The Motif Night as Danger Associated with Three Biblical Destruction Narratives." In *Sha'arei Talmon: Studies in the Bible, Qumran, and the Ancient Near*

East Presented to Shemaryahu Talmon, edited by Michael Fishbane et al., 17–32. Winona Lake, IN: Eisenbaum, 1992.

Fitzmyer, Joseph A. "Tobit." In *Qumran Cave 4. XIV. Parabiblical Texts Part 2*, edited by Magen Broshi et al., 1–76. DJD 19. Oxford: Clarendon, 1995.

———. *Tobit*. CEJL. Berlin: de Gruyter, 2003.

Frey-Anthes, Henrike. "Praise, Petition, Lament—and Back: On the Significance of Lament in the Book of Tobit." In *Evoking Lament: A Theological Discussion*, edited by Eva Harasta and Brian Brock, 136–49. London: T. & T. Clark, 2009.

Fröhlich, Ida. "Tobit against the Background of the Dead Sea Scrolls." In *The Book of Tobit: Text, Tradition, Theology*, edited by Geza G. Xeravits and Jozsef Zsengeller, 55–70. JSJSup 98. Leiden: Brill, 2005.

Gafni, Isaiah. *Land, Center and Diaspora: Jewish Constructs in Late Antiquity*. JSPSup 21. Sheffield: Sheffield Academic, 1997.

———. "Reinterment in the Land of Israel: Notes on the Origin and Development of the Custom." In *The Jerusalem Cathedra*, edited by Lee I. Levine, 96–104. Studies in the History, Archeology, Geography and Ethnography of the Land of Israel 1. Jerusalem: Izhak Ben-Zvi Institute, 1981.

Garland, Robert. *The Greek Way of Death*. 2nd ed. Ithaca, NY: Cornell University Press, 2001.

Haag, Ernst. "Das Tobitbuch und die Tradition von Jahweh, dem Heiler Israels (Ex 15,26)." *Trierer Theologische Zeitschrift* 111 (2002) 23–41.

Hachlili, Rachel. *Jewish Funerary Customs, Practices and Rites in the Second Temple Period*. JSJSup 94. Leiden: Brill, 2005.

Hallote, Rachel S. *Death, Burial, and Afterlife in the Biblical World: How the Israelites and Their Neighbors Treated the Dead*. Chicago: Dee, 2001.

Hanhart, Robert, ed. *Tobit*. Septuaginta Vetus Testamentum Graecum VIII.5. Göttingen: Vandenhoeck & Ruprecht, 1983.

Harrison, Robert P. *The Dominion of the Dead*. Chicago: University of Chicago Press, 2003.

Hayward, C. T. Robert. "*Multum in Parvo*: Ben Sira's Portrayal of the Patriarch Joseph." In *Intertextual Studies in Ben Sira and Tobit: Essays in Honor of Alexander A. Di Lella OFM*, edited by Jeremy Corley and Vincent Skemp, 185–200. CBQMS 38. Washington, DC: Catholic Biblical Association of America, 2004.

Hicks-Keeton, Jill. "Already/Not Yet: Eschatological Tension in the Book of Tobit." *JBL* 132 (2013) 97–117.

Jensen, Hans J. L. "Family, Fertility and Foul Smell: Tobit and Judith." In *Studies in the Book of Tobit: A Multidisciplinary Approach*, edited by Mark Bredin, 129–39. LSTS 55. London: T. & T. Clark, 2006.

Johnston, Philip S. *Shades of Sheol: Death and Afterlife in the Old Testament*. Downers Grove, IL: Intervarsity, 2002.

Kiel, Micah D. "Tobit and Moses Redux." *JSP* 17 (2008) 83–98.

———. "Tobit's Theological Blindness." *CBQ* 73 (2011) 281–98.

———. *The "Whole Truth": Rethinking Retribution in the Book of Tobit*. LSTS 82. London: T. & T. Clark, 2012.

Kierkegaard, Søren. *Fear and Trembling*. Translated by Alastair Hannay. New York: Penguin, 2006.

Kottsieper, Ingo. "'Look Son, What Nadab Did to Ahikaros . . .': The Aramaic Ahiqar Tradition and Its Relationship to the Book of Tobit." In *The Dynamics of Language and Exegesis at Qumran*, edited by Devorah Dimant and Reinhard G. Kratz, 145–67. Forschungen zum Alten Testament 2/35. Tübingen: Mohr/Siebeck, 2009.

Kugel, James L. *In Potiphar's House: The Interpretive Life of Biblical Texts*. Cambridge: Harvard University Press, 1994.

Lakoff, George, and Mark Johnson. *Metaphors We Live By*. Chicago: University of Chicago Press, 1980.

Levenson, Jon D. *Resurrection and the Restoration of Israel: The Ultimate Victory of the God of Life*. New Haven: Yale University Press, 2006.

Levine, Amy-Jill. "Diaspora as Metaphor: Bodies and Boundaries in the Book of Tobit." In *Diaspora Jews and Judaism: Essays in Honor of, and in Dialogue with, A. Thomas Kraabel*, edited by J. Andrew Overman and Robert S. MacLennan, 105–17. South Florida Studies in the History of Judaism 41. Atlanta: University of South Florida Press, 1992.

Liddell, H. H., and R. Scott. "ἀποκαθαίρω." In *Greek-English Lexicon with a Revised Supplement*, 200. 9th ed. Oxford: Clarendon, 1996.

Littman, Robert J. Tobit. *The Book of Tobit in Codex Sinaiticus*. SCS. Leiden: Brill, 2008.

Macatangay, Francis M. "Acts of Charity as Acts of Remembrance in the Book of Tobit." *JSP* 23 (2013) 69–84.

———. "Apocalypticism and Narration in the Book of Tobit." In *Canonicity, Setting, Wisdom in the Deuterocanonicals*, edited by Geza G. Xeravits et al., 207–20. DCLSt 22. Berlin: de Gruyter, 2014.

———. "Election by Allusion: Exodus Themes in the Book of Tobit." *CBQ* 76 (2014) 450–63.

———. "Exile as Metaphor in the Book of Tobit." *Rivista Biblica Italiana* 70 (2014) 177–92.

———. "Metaphors and the Character Construction of Tobias in the Book of Tobit." In *The Metaphorical Use of Language in Deuterocanonical and Cognate Literature*, edited by Markus Witte and Sven Behnke, 75–86. Deuterocanonical and Cognate Literature Yearbook 2014/2015. Berlin: de Gruyter, 2015.

———. "Μισθός and Irony in the Book of Tobit." *Bib* 94 (2013) 576–84.

———. "The Wisdom Discourse of Tobit as Instruction in Torah." *BN* 167 (2015) 99–111.

———. *The Wisdom Instructions in the Book of Tobit*. DCLSt 12. Berlin: de Gruyter, 2011.

Machiela, Daniel A. and Perrin, Andrew A. "Tobit and the *Genesis Apocryphon*: Toward a Family Portrait." *JBL* 133 (2014) 111–32.

MacDonald, Nathan. "'Bread on the Grave of the Righteous' (Tob 4:17)." In *Studies in the Book of Tobit: A Multidisciplinary Approach*, edited by Mark Bredin, 99–103. LSTS 55. London: T. & T. Clark, 2006.

McCane, Byron R. "Death and Burial, Hellenistic and Roman Period, Palestine." In *The Oxford Encyclopedia of the Bible and Archaeology*, edited by Daniel M. Master, 1:262–70. Oxford: Oxford University Press, 2013.

———. *Roll Back the Stone: Death and Burial in the World of Jesus*. Harrisburg, PA: Trinity, 2003.

McCracken, David. "Narration and Comedy in the Book of Tobit." *JBL* 114 (1995) 401–18.

Meyers, Carol. *Discovering Eve: Ancient Israelite Women in Context*. Oxford: Oxford University Press, 1988.

Meyers, Eric M. *Jewish Ossuaries: Reburial and Rebirth*. BO 24. Rome: Pontifical Biblical Institute Press, 1971.

Miller, Geoffrey D. *Marriage in the Book of Tobit*. DCLSt 10. Berlin: de Gruyter, 2011.

————. "Raphael the Liar: Angelic Deceit and Testing in the Book of Tobit." *CBQ* 74 (2012) 492–508.

Moore, Carey A. *Tobit: A New Translation with Introduction and Commentary.* AB 40A. New York: Doubleday, 1996.

Nickelsburg, George W. E. *Jewish Literature between the Bible and the Mishnah: A Historical and Literary Introduction.* 2nd ed. Minneapolis: Fortress, 2005.

————. "The Search for Tobit's Mixed Ancestry: A Historical and Hermeneutical Odyssey." *RevQ* 17 (1996) 339–49.

————. "Tobit." In *Harper's Bible Commentary*, edited by James L. Mays, 791–803. San Francisco: Harper & Row, 1988.

Nicklas, Tobias. "Denn der Herr kennt den Weg der Gerechten . . . (Ps 1,6a): Lesespaziergänge vom Buch Tobit in der Psalter." *SJOT* 19 (2005) 61–73.

Novick, Tzvi. "Biblicized Narrative: On Tobit and Genesis 22." *JBL* 126 (2007) 755–64.

Nowell, Irene. "The Book of Tobit: An Ancestral Story." In *Intertextual Studies in Ben Sira and Tobit: Essays in Honor of Alexander A. Di Lella OFM*, edited by Jeremy Corely and Vincent Skemp, 3–13. CBQMS 38. Washington, DC: CBA, 2005.

————. "The Book of Tobit: Narrative Technique and Theology." PhD diss., Catholic University of America, 1983.

————. "The Narrator in the Book of Tobit." In *SBL 1988 Seminar Series*, edited by David J. Lull, 27–38. Atlanta: Scholar, 1988.

Oeming, Manfred. "Jewish Identity in the Eastern Diaspora in Light of the Book of Tobit." In *Judah and the Judeans in the Achaemenid Period: Negotiating Identity in an International Context*, edited by Oded Lipschits et al., 545–61. Winona Lake, IN: Eisenbrauns, 2011.

Olyan, Saul. "Some Neglected Aspects of Israelite Interment Ideology." *JBL* 124 (2005) 601–16.

Otzen, Benedikt. *Tobit and Judith.* Guides to Apocrypha and Pseudepigrapha. London: Sheffield Academic, 2002.

Perrin, Andrew B. "Tobit's Context and Contacts in the Qumran Aramaic Anthology." *JSP* 25 (2015) 23–51.

————. "An Almanac of Tobit Studies: 2000–2014." *Currents in Biblical Research* 13 (2014) 107–42.

Petraglio, Renzo. "Tobit e Anna: un cammino difficile nella crisi di una coppia." *Rivista Biblica Italiana* 52 (2004) 385–402.

Pitkänen, Pekka. "Family Life and Ethnicity in Early Israel and in Tobit." In *Studies in the Book of Tobit: A Multidisciplinary Approach*, edited by Mark Bredin, 104–17. LSTS 55. London: T. & T. Clark, 2006.

Portier-Young, Anathea. "Alleviation of Suffering in the Book of Tobit: Comedy, Community, and Happy Endings." *CBQ* 63 (2001) 35–54.

————. "Eyes to the Blind: A Dialogue between Tobit and Job." In *Intertextual Studies in Ben Sira and Tobit: Essays in Honor of Alexander A. Di Lella OFM*, edited by Jeremy Corley and Vincent Skemp, 14–27. CBQMS 38. Washington, DC: CBA, 2005.

Priero, Giuseppe. *Tobia.* La Sacra Bibbia. Torino: Marietti, 1953.

Pyper, Hugh. "'Sarah is the Hero': Kierkegaard's Reading of Tobit in *Fear and Trembling*." In *Studies in the Book of Tobit: A Multidisciplinary Approach*, edited by Mark Bredin, 59–71. LSTS 55. London: T. & T. Clark, 2006.

Quarles, Charles L. "New Perspective and Atonement in Jewish Literature of the Second Temple Period." *Criswell Theological Review* 2 (2005) 39–56.

Rabenau, Merten. *Studien zum Buch Tobit.* BZAW 220. Berlin: de Gruyter, 1994.

Rauntenberg, Johanna. *Verlässlikchkeit des Wortes: Gemeinschaftskonzepte in den Reden des Buches Tobit und ihre Legitimierung.* Bonner Biblische Beiträge 176. Göttingen: Vandenhoeck & Ruprecht, 2015.

Ravasi, Gianfranco. "Il cantico della misericordia (Tb 13)." *Parola spirito e vita* 29 (1994) 73–84.

Rosenthal, Franz. "Sedaka, Charity." *HUCA* 23 (1950–51) 411–30.

Roth, Philip. *Everyman.* Boston: Houghton Mifflin, 2006.

Ruppert, Lothar. "Das Buch Tobias—ein Modelfall nachgestaltender Erzählung." In *Wort, Lied und Gottespruch: Beiträge zur Septuaginta. Festschrift für Joseph Ziegler,* edited by Josef Schreiner, 109–19. Forschung zur Bibel 1–2. Würzburg: Echter, 1972.

Schellenberg, Ryan. "Suspense, Simultaneity, and Divine Providence in the Book of Tobit." *JBL* 130 (2011) 313–27.

Schumpp, Meinrad M. *Das Buch Tobias.* Exegetisches Handbuch zum Alten Testament 11. Münster: Aschendorff, 1933.

Schüngel-Straumann, Helen. *Tobit.* Herders Theologischer Kommentar zum Alten Testament. Freiburg: Herder, 2000.

Schwartz, Jacques. "Remarques littéraire sur le roman de Tobit." *RHPR* 67 (1987) 293–97.

Skemp, Vincent. "Ἀδελφός and the Theme of Kinship in Tobit." *ETL* 75 (1999) 92–103.

———. *The Vulgate of Tobit Compared with Other Ancient Witnesses.* SBLDS 180. Atlanta: SBL, 2000.

Soll, Will. "The Book of Tobit as a Window on the Hellenistic Jewish Family." In *Passion, Vitality, and Foment: The Dynamics of Second Temple Judaism,* edited by Lamontte M. Luker, 242–74. Harrisburg, PA: Trinity, 2001.

———. "Misfortune and Exile in Tobit: The Juncture of a Fairy Tale Source and Deuteronomic Theology." *CBQ* 51 (1989) 209–31.

Stavrakopoulou, Francesca. *Land of Our Fathers: The Roles of Ancestor Veneration in Biblical Land Claims.* LHBOTS 473. London: T. & T. Clark, 2012.

Stemm, Sönke von. *Der betende Sünder vor Gott: Studien zu Vergebungsvorstellungen in urchristlichen und frühjüdischen Texten.* Arbeiten zur Geschichte des antiken Judentums und des Urchristentums 45. Leiden: Brill, 1999.

Stern, Karen B. "Death and Burial in the Jewish Diaspora." In *The Oxford Encyclopedia of the Bible and Archaeology,* edited by Daniel M. Master, 1:270–80. Oxford: Oxford University Press, 2013.

Tromp, Nicholas J. *Primitive Concepts of Death and the Nether World in the Old Testament.* BO 21. Rome: Pontifical Biblical Institute, 1969.

Unnik, Willem C. van. *Das Selbstverständnis der jüdischen Diaspora in der hellenistisch-römischen Zeit.* Arbeiten zur Geschichte des antiken Judentums und des Urchristentums 17. Leiden: Brill 1993.

Vaux, Roland de. *Ancient Israel: Its Life and Institutions.* Translated by John McHugh. New York: McGraw-Hill, 1961.

Vilchez, Jose. *Tobias y Judit.* Narraciones 3. Estella, Navarra: Verbo Divino, 2000.

Wagner, Christian J., ed. *Polyglotte Tobit-Synopse: Griechisch—Lateinisch—Syrisch—Hebräisch—Aramäisch. Mit einem Index zu den Tobit-Fragmenten vom Toten Meer.* Abhandlungen der Akademie der Wissenschaften in Göttingen Philologisch-Historische Klasse 258. Göttingen: Vandenhoeck & Ruprecht, 2003.

Weeks, Stuart. "A Deuteronomic Heritage in Tobit." In *Changes in Scripture: Rewriting and Interpreting Authoritative Traditions in the Second Temple*, edited by Hanne von Weissenberg et al., 389–403. BZAW 419. Berlin: de Gruyter, 2011.

———. "Reconstructing Tobit 13:6–10." In *The Temple in Text and Tradition: A Festschrift in Honor of Robert Hayward*, edited by R. Timothy McLay, 35–47. LSTS 83. London: T. & T. Clark, 2015.

———. "Restoring the Greek Tobit." *JSJ* 24 (2013) 1–15.

Weeks, Stuart et al., eds. *Tobit: Texts from the Principal Ancient and Medieval Traditions. With Synopsis, Concordances, and Annotated Texts in Aramaic, Hebrew, Greek, Latin and Syriac.* FoSub 3. Berlin: de Gruyter, 2004.

Weigl, Michael. "Die rettende Macht der Barmherzigkeit. Achikar im Buch Tobit." *BZ* 50 (2006) 212–43.

Weitzman, Steven. "Allusion, Artifice, and Exile in the Hymn of Tobit." *JBL* 115 (1996) 49–61.

Wills, Lawrence M. *The Jewish Novel in the Ancient World.* 1995. Reprinted, Eugene, OR: Wipf & Stock, 2015.

Zanella, Francesco. "Between Righteousness and Alms: A Semantic Study of the Lexeme צדקה in the Dead Sea Scrolls." In *Hebrew in the Second Temple Period: The Hebrew of the Dead Sea Scrolls and of Other Contemporary Sources*, edited by Steven E. Fassberg et al., 269–87. Studies on the Texts of the Desert of Judah 108. Leiden: Brill, 2013.

Zappella, Marco. *Tobit: Introduzione, traduzione e commento.* Nuova versione della bibbia dai testi antichi 30. Cinisello Balsamo: San Paolo, 2010.

Zimmermann, Frank. *The Book of Tobit.* Jewish Apocryphal Literature. New York: Harper, 1958.

Index of Modern Authors

Index of References

Daniel
4:24	37, 41

Amos
2:6	3

Micah
4:1–2	35

Haggai
2:13	57

Zechariah
8:21–22	35

Tobit
1–2	50, 56
1:1	10
1:1–2	10, 11, 66
1:2	10
1:3	9, 11, 29, 86
1:4	71
1:6	23
1:8	22, 51, 62
1:10	10, 11, 88
1:11	23, 36
1:14–15	12
1:15	12, 32
1:16–20	2
1:16–18	29
1:17	48, 66
1:18–20	14, 59
1:18	13, 48, 59
1:19	12
1:20	4
1:22	12, 26, 35
2–12	5
2:1–10	48
2:1–8	2, 25
2:1–5	40
2:1	4, 14, 26
2:2	24, 35, 51

2:3–7	14
2:4	67
2:7–9	50
2:7	67
2:8	13
2:9–14	25
2:10	26, 30, 35
2:14	38
3:1–6	13, 19, 25
3:2	22, 86
3:2–6	12
3:3–5	41
3:3–4	41
3:3	88
3:4	10, 13, 60
3:6	4, 10, 14, 19, 61
3:7–10	16
3:7–9	13
3:9–10	14
3:11	22
3:14–15	16
3:15	16, 21
3:17	21, 22, 82
4	6, 43
4:1–21	52
4:1–2	61
4:2	77
4:3–21	24
4:3	2, 49
4:4–11	32
4:4–6	25
4:4	3, 37, 53, 58, 66, 68
4:5	36
4:6	25, 35, 51, 81
4:7–11	30
4:7–8	3, 37
4:7	31, 85, 86
4:8–9	31
4:10	25, 31, 37, 40, 49, 79
4:11	31, 38, 81
4:12	72
4:16–17	30
4:16	3, 37
4:17	51, 66
4:19	19, 25, 40, 83